Following the Trade

Tom Foxon

Following the Trade
Copyright Tom Foxon 2010

ISBN 978-0-905366-40-1

First published in 2010

The Tom Foxon Trilogy –

Anderton for Orders
Number One
Following the Trade

Cover design by David Miller

Prepared for press by Robert Wilson Designs

Printed for and published by

THE BELMONT PRESS   020-8907 4700
29 Tenby Avenue   Harrow   HA3 8RU
                FAX 020-8907 7354

Following the Trade

The Author

Tom Foxon was born in 1933, not far from the Grand Union Canal in Heston, Middlesex. He left his first job in an insurance office at the age of 16 to work as a mate on a canal boat.

Following three years service in the RAF he successfully traded as an owner-boatman until 1959 when he sold out and became a Captain in the British Waterways Midland Fleet. There his contact with bargemen on the River Severn lead him to give up canal boating and spend the next few years working on river and estuarial craft.

Three years after his marriage in 1963 (his wife Jeanne worked on a horse-drawn hostel boat for some years in the late 1950's) Tom 'swallowed the anchor' and following a period as a lock-keeper went to work on the railways; firstly as a guard and then as a signalman in the Worcester area.

Imbued with a lifelong fascination with transport and industrial land-scapes, Tom Foxon is a member of the Railway and Canal Historical Society, contributes articles to waterways magazines and gives talks to societies.

The Belmont Press
www.the-belmont-press.co.uk

Other titles by Tom Foxon

His Trilogy –

Anderton for Orders
Number One
Following the Trade

Tom Foxon - Following the Trade -

Tom's life as a working boatman

The year is 1954 and, fresh from National Service, Tom Foxon has become a 'Number One', the owner and captain of a working narrowboat with which he is determined to trade as far and wide as the canal system will allow.

First, though. While his boat *New Hope* is being docked at Tamworth, he joins legendary Ray White in an episode of horse-boating between Worcester and the Black Country.

Then, with his own boat freshly docked and ready for work, Tom does a spell trading to' Longford Light' power station at Coventry, before heading north to the Potteries, where he picks up a load of gravel destined for Manchester.

His next cargo is a shipment of metal loaded overside from a ship in Manchester dock and carried by way of the Shropshire Union to Birmingham. Engine problems cause considerable delay and Ton is forced to the realisation that *New Hope* must have a costly new engine sooner rather than later.

To generate some funds he commences work in the more lucrative, short haul environment of the Birmingham Canal Navigations and we are treated to evocative accounts of an ice bound winter spent with Joey boats at such salubrious locations as 'Saltley Sidings' and 'Moxley tip'! Deep down, however, Tom's concept of perfect boating is set in more rural landscapes than the Black Country and the final chapters of 'Number One' find him idyllically engaged on the Oxford Canal with cargoes of coal to Oxford and Banbury.

ILLUSTRATIONS

CONTENTS

CHAPTER ONE

Oxford Weed and Coventry Coal

Anyone alighting from an early train at Aynho and pausing on the adjacent bridge over the Oxford Canal on a fine June morning in 1955 might have been lucky enough to see an Oxford bound coal boat pass underneath. Her paintwork might have shown the patina of wear but, observing her polished brasses, scrubbed woodwork and generally neat and tidy appearance and savouring the tempting aroma of frying bacon wafting upwards from her cabin, our observer might well have thought to himself "What a wonderful life!"

Had he been on the canalside somewhere around Kidlington on the following day he might have changed his mind. The approaching boat would have been heralded by the sound of a labouring engine and a cloud of black smoke. As it struggled painfully past he would see the steerer bend down every minute or so to pull back his reverse rod, open up the engine sharply astern, then put it back into forward gear. And why was the boat stopping in every bridgehole while the steerer stepped off and groped under the counter with a shaft?

The answer came when the shaft was withdrawn, a huge ball of green on its hook. The blanket weed season had arrived!

The weed had started somewhere below Heyford. I had left Banbury that morning with 23 ½ tons of coal from Griff colliery in Warwickshire bound for Morrell's Brewery at Oxford. Twelve and a half hours later I had only got as far as the Pigeons pub near Kirtlington, sixteen miles covered at an average of one and a half miles an hour.

The next day was even worse. From the Pigeons to Duke's lock is eight miles. It took me seven exhausting hours, wreathed in black exhaust smoke, worrying about the strain on the gearbox, continually "chucking back" (that is alternately reversing the engine and going ahead again) in an attempt to throw the weed of the blades and getting off in every bridge hole to delve under the counter with the shaft. It was exhausting work. First the sharp point of the shaft had to be rammed into the mass of weed between the weed and the shafting. Then you had to give a series of violent forward jerks to loosen the weed on the propshaft. Having done this the point was withdrawn and the weed seized with the hook. More jerking followed in an attempt to pull away the weed. It was wasted effort; as soon as the engine was put in gear it immediately picked up another bladeful. All attempts at keeping the boat and cabin tidy went by the board as the unequal battle continued through the day.

The three miles from Duke's to the wharf at Juxon Street in Oxford took two and a quarter hours.

I was the only boat trading to Oxford at the time but I knew some old boatmen around those parts and I asked them what to do. The answer was "Bowhaul!" I could imagine this being done if there was someone to steer while I pulled but I was working singlehanded and this meant that the boat would have to be shafted from the bank. I knew that boats had been moved quite long distances by pushing with a shaft from the towpath. Shafting was a routine operation around Birmingham and it was one of the many skills that boatmen had to acquire. One boatman used to shaft loaded boats from Sandwell colliery near West Bromwich to the copper works at Selly Oak on the Worcester cut, a distance of five and a half miles. But this was on a well maintained route. Obviously the idea of trying to shaft a loaded boat along a cut where you were often ploughing through mud was impracticable.

Morrell's coal was a subcontract for S. E. Barlow, a once large carrier based at Glascote on the outskirts of Tamworth but now reduced to a handful of boats, a dockyard, a retail coal round and some coal factoring. I rang up "S.E." and told him of the situation. I was told "Not to worry, there's plenty of work to the Light (Longford Power Station) and Morrell's can go by train".

At the time I was disappointed at having to withdraw from the Oxford run because I had felt a lot of satisfaction in getting some trade to Oxford back on the water. Having painfully ploughed a channel through the accumulated scours and settled down to a cosy routine I was loath to be defeated. Reflecting on the situation later I was forced to admit to myself that, what with the extremely slow going below Banbury, the delays caused by floods in winter and weed in summer and the isolation of being the only boat trading below Banbury, I might sooner or later have become fed up with confining myself to this particular job although it would always be nice to have the occasional trip down there.

Nor was I very keen on going back onto the Longford Light run. I had done this job before and considered it poorly paid, boring and excessively dirty. It would have to do until something more attractive turned up so, having emptied my load of coal at Juxon Street, I set off back to Pooley Hall Colliery picking up no small amount of weed which I had disturbed on my way down and which was now floating on the surface.

Readers of my earlier book "No. One" will recall that the run between Pooley Hall and Longford Light had been my first job as an owner boatman. The power station, which was situated on the Oxford Canal about half a mile from Hawkesbury Junction had been built to replace an earlier and smaller power station at Harnall Lane on the Coventry Canal originally built to supply power to the city's trams. It was equipped with two unloading telfers (grabs on gantries) and had received an enormous amount of coal by canal in its earlier days. The water borne proportion of total consumption had declined year by year since the war, the long freeze-up of 1947 having affected the canal trade badly, and by the summer of 1955 only four boats a day were being unloaded. The coal came from collieries at Pooley and Measham and was supplemented by a trainload each day. The remainder was carried in the ever increasing lorry fleet of the Samuel Barlow Coal Co. whose boats handled the Measham part of the traffic.

One reason why the job was poorly paid was because the Light would unload no more than four boats each day thus causing delays in unloading.. On the other hand they would not accept averaging but demanded no LESS than four boats daily despite the machinery allowing canal borne to be put to stock and that they regularly drew from stock so as to turn the stockpile over gradually and not allow any old coal to remain there too long.

This meant that the carriers had to employ more boats on the job than would have been needed had more flexible unloading arrangements obtained. Without the unloading delays it would have been easy to do three trips per week; as it was, only two trips were possible. The rate I was paid at that time was 4s 6d (22p) per ton so it can be seen that two trips of 23 tons earned £10. 7s whereas three trips would have earned £15. 10s 6d. The latter figure would have been regarded as quite satisfactory by comparison with other canal jobs so it can be seen just how much our incomes were affected by unloading delays. Subcontractors were always told not to tell anyone what they were being paid but one day I happened, quite casually, to mention the rate to Joe Skinner only to discover that I was being paid more than him. Of course, the Skinners had a row with "S. E." about this and I got told off by his dragon-like secretary for not keeping quiet. I couldn't understand why we were not both paid the same for the same job and I was pleased that I had been responsible for righting an obvious injustice.

Barlow's lorries, of course, suffered no such delays. Oh no! They drove up, deposited their loads on the stockpile and disappeared in a cloud of dust. Coal from the boats and trains went directly into the power station. Anyone who has read that excellent book by Sir John Knill, "John Knill's Navy", will encounter many a heartfelt complaint about delays to boats while lorries arrived and were dealt with immediately. By this time, Sir John, then plain Mr Knill, was the boat manager for the Samuel Barlow Coal company, having recently had to liquidate his carrying business. In the event, the Light job turned out better than expected and even became quite enjoyable. Pooley was a good place to load, the coal coming down to the wharf in railway trucks to which a hoist was attached, lifting one end of the wagon and allowing the coal to run into a hopper. A large iron lever admitted coal to the boat's hold and the operation was quick and could be carefully controlled. I had loaded at Pooley many times before and knew the boatloaders, George and Ernie, well. After the first trip I experimented with increasing the load and found that I could carry at least 24 tons over this route. My biggest load to the light was 25 tons 3cwt. The extra 10s or so each week on my earnings was very welcome.

With this sort of load her hold was completely full, piled up as high as it would go from the back end to the middle beam, a good pile in front of the mast and level between the mast and the middle beam. With wooden boats it was always a good idea to leave them light behind the mast as it was reckoned to keep the transverse three inch elm bottoms closed up, preventing leaks.

Deep in the water like this, planks up on the stands, cratch decorated with scrubbed canvas belt and snowy white cotton line, she looked really good and, on many an evening when I had tied up above Atherstone locks, I would stand on the opposite bank puffing a contemplative cigarette, lost in admiration of her beautiful lines!

Once loaded and cleaned up, the engine started and a cup of tea on the slide in front of me, I would set off. It is about four miles from Pooley to Atherstone bottom lock and it was slow going, taking two hours, the throttle just cracked open to avoid sucking the water away round the boat and dropping her on the bottom of the cut, but the surroundings were quiet and remote and the countryside pleasant. The only village on this part of the canal was Polesworth where Lees & Atkins had a boat dock. Sometimes I would tie up here when I was coming down empty and was too late to load at the colliery and join Jim Atkins for a drink in the Royal Oak. There was also a cinema here in the former Polesworth Mill, notable for its double seat "hug-me-tights" in the back rows.

Atherstone locks, two at the bottom, a long pound, then two at Baddesley, another long pound and five from Watling Street bridge to the top were the slowest I ever encountered as they were not fitted with top gate paddles. They did have side pounds which added little to the speed of operation. One Saturday as I was locking down at the bottom lock I encountered a group of youths from the nearby mining village of Baddesley carrying towels and swimming trunks. They stopped and watched the boat go through the lock and I asked them if they were going to swim in the cut. It turned out that their swimming place was in the nearby river Anker. I was curious, having done a lot of river swimming in my schooldays when there used to be long queues for the public baths so I tied my empty boat up below the bottom lock and joined them. It was a nice place to swim, clean water and secluded by bushes. A handy swimming hole, only a stone's throw from the cut, was useful to know about, especially as we were enjoying a spell of very hot weather.

George Beechy was the lock keeper for the lower part of the Atherstone flight and lived in a cottage at the bottom lock. The cut remained shallow up to the lock by Baddesley Colliery basin, a busy place where boats were loaded for various destinations on the Oxford, Birmingham and Grand Union canals. Baddesley coal was of very good quality and I would always try to top up the supply in my back end bunker if I could. The quarter of a mile, tree shaded, pound above Baddesley brings you to Watling Street, a handy place to tie up if you wanted to stop at Atherstone. Here began the last five locks of the flight, all close together and supervised by a Mr Earp, known, as might be expected, as "Wyatt".

Atherstone top lock was a popular place to tie up going south, you had a long, lock free pound to start the day's work in the morning and it was close to the shops and those essential amenities for boatmen, a pub, fish and chips and the "pictures".

The eleven mile pound from Atherstone to Sutton's Stop was slightly deeper and took four and a half hours, not a very good speed considering that the difficult eleven mile summit of the Oxford Canal could be done in 10 minutes less. The first four miles were very pleasant, winding past Mancetter, where boats loaded with roadstone and there was a good tie up and pub, and the canal maintenance depot at Hartshill to Boon's Stone Quarry, the first of several between here and Griff. The cut was much shallower here, choked with the runoff from the quarry washing plants, and wound through the rather dreary outskirts of Nuneaton, an unexciting town quite a long walk from the cut. At Coton there was another good place to tie up, and here the canal re-entered rural countryside, passing the junction of the Griff Colliery Arm, the junction with the Ashby canal at Marston, and Charity boat dock before reaching the Newdigate Colliery Arm on the outskirts of Bedworth. There was always a lot of activity here, with many boats tied up outside the pub in which I spent many an enjoyable evening.

The only attraction at Bedworth, apart from the local girls, was a roller skating rink patronised by many of the younger boatman.

Passing the wharf where Courtauld's rubbish boats unloaded, you finally came to Sutton's Stop with its stop place on the Coventry canal, toll and boat control offices, nasty 180 degree turn and six inch fall stop lock between the two canals, not forgetting the Greyhound pub and shop where you could refuel yourself and your boat.

There was an unwritten agreement that boats could tie up at Sutton's, instead of going round to the Light and waiting there amidst all the coal dust, and still retain their turn for unloading and the delays in unloading meant that I often spent the weekend here. The Greyhound was run by Ron, Mary and Rowena Nelson. It was a busy pub, with the bar crowded at night. The quarried stone floors and scrubbed tables were typical of canal pubs in an age that has now vanished. There was no bar counter but orders were taken and drinks brought to you There was a shop attached, which was useful, but to buy meat, paraffin or methylated spirits a trip had to be made to Longford a mile away. From Longford there was a bus service into Coventry. A horse drawn vegetable cart visited Sutton's a couple of times a week.

The nearest "pictures" was also at Longford and here I must digress and explain that, in those days, the cinema was a vital place for meeting girls. How it worked was that the girls would go to the pictures with their mates but sit by themselves. A boy would then enquire if the girl was by herself and, if the answer was "yes", would ask if he could sit next to her. If the girl agreed it was expected that, as soon as the lights went down and the film started, cuddling and kissing would ensue. Behind the pictures was an extent of waste land and bushes, now Longford Park, where, after the show, lads and lasses could continue to enjoy each other's company.

After I had done my first trip to the power station I had orders to go to Griff and load house coal for Rugby Co-op. This was an exceptionally well paid and much coveted job the rate for which was 7s per ton plus 2s 6d for shovelling out the coal. This trip was memorable for the fact that I started from Sutton's extremely early as we were having a spell of very hot July weather, only to encounter a thick morning fog. In spite of this I was at Rugby by 8.30am ready to start shovelling before the heat of the day. The wharf was at the end of the Rugby arm, which was a truncated loop of the original line of the Oxford Canal. There was nothing else here except the remains of the railway wharf opposite where, in former days, east midland coal was transhipped from railway wagon to boats. In the 1840's, merchandise traffic had also been interchanged here. The water in the arm was deep and clear so that you could see the bottom of the cut.

The wharf was a "shelf" wharf, that is the road was lower than the cut and the wharf was level with the height of a lorry platform, so that coal could be bagged and easily loaded onto a lorry without lifting. I set to with a will, having left the usual "break" so that I could start shovelling on the floorboards, but as with most wharves, space was restricted and I soon found myself throwing the coal up on top of a mountain that had accumulated. As long as you are shovelling right handed, i.e. toward the fore end of the boat in this case, it is not too bad, but when you had to turn round and shovel left handed towards the back of the hold, the part which held the most coal, it became painfully slow. This monotonous work was only relieved by the occasional passage of a steam train on the Rugby to Leicester branch line.

By noon I had had enough. I stripped off and dived into the cut to remove the coating of coal dust, and having made myself reasonably presentable, went in search of beer. The nearest pub proved to be a long way down the road, and although Joules Ale (brewed at Stone) was not particularly to my taste, I enjoyed several pints before returning to the boat where I had a sandwich, followed by a sleep. By four pm the heat had started to go out of the day and I spent most of the evening shovelling, finishing off early next morning to be back in time for a lunchtime drink in the Greyhound.

Trading to the Light resumed, it's monotony only being broken when I was delayed loaded at Suttons for the weekend when I would sometimes accompany one of my old friends, Ray White, who worked for the "Limited", part of the way on his trip down the "Junction", on one occasion getting as far as Fenny Stratford. It made a change to be on a pair of boats and to be able to exercise the skills of working through wide locks. Ray had the Tiger and Jane at that time and the Tiger's 12hp single cylinder Petter was the only one I ever had the opportunity to drive. Compared to a Bolinder 'big engine' they were weak but shared the Bolinder's advantage of extreme reliability.

How I spent the colliery holiday I can't remember but it caused a gap in loading between the 21st of July and the 10th of August. Boatmen didn't go away on holidays, contenting themselves with a few day trips.

At the end of August I received orders to load coal for the Thames Conservancy at Oxford and, loading the following day in the Newdigate arm, got as far as Braunston that night. The following day I encountered low pounds all the way and it took me twelve and a half hours to get as far as Jobson's lock, the second one above Banbury. The weed season was over but the going was as difficult as ever between Banbury and Oxford. To deliver the coal to the Thames Conservancy yard at Osney meant going out on the river so I first had to visit the London Midland Region station at Rewley Road and arrange for the railway swing bridge to be opened, the delay meaning that I didn't get to Osney until 10am. Nevertheless a gang of Conservancy men had New Hope unloaded by 3pm and I got back above Louse lock for the night.

For company on the Light run I had Dick Littlemore and Bill Humphries, both working for S. E. Barlow. They were both Oxford men exiled, so to speak, by the decline of the Oxford trade. The Samuel Barlow Coal Co., known more conveniently as the "Limited", used any of their boats on their contract from Measham and I was often in the company of my old friends Ray White and Ted Barratt. Ray had started his boating career as a Number One, later worked with me for John Knill and on the British Waterways North Western Division Eagle, had a previous spell with the Limited and several years in charge of a Charles Ballinger horse boat. Ted Barratt, about my own age, and his brother Ken were the two oldest of the large Barratt family, his parents also working for Barlow's. Father and son were famous as "Bolinder men", quite capable of stripping those engines down to the bed plate and rebuilding them. His fondness for playing with engines earned Ted junior the nickname "Sooty".

It was during that summer of 1955 that Dick Littlemore retired and his boats were taken over by Ben Johnson, another old Oxford boatman. Ben dressed in the same old fashioned clothes as Joe Skinner, a style that had been long abandoned by everyone else on the cut. He wasn't often seen on the Light run because Alf Townsend, who was getting on in years and who worked a British Waterways pair two-handed with his nephew Wilf, had come to an arrangement whereby his boats would be hired to S. E. Barlow. Two trips a week from Pooley to Longford light was easy compared with working shorthanded on the Junction with its heavy locks and heavy traffic. The Townsends hailed from Abingdon and the family had once owned its own boats. Wilf would boast of his Teddy-boy suit but I never saw him wearing it.

S.E. needed an extra pair on his Home Park paper mill contract and that suited Ben very well. He was obsessed with having his top planks exactly straight and level and was always fiddling about with bits of wood and wedges. The rest of us found Ben's preoccupation amusing and would gather round offering advice. It was all good natured fun. Ben was one of the few boatmen who I have actually seen clog dancing on a table top.

When Dick retired he offered me the chance to buy his entire collection of brass knobs and hanging up plates for a mere three pounds. There were three fine knobs, screwed onto a backplate, two brass rods that were hung over the range and enough plates to make the traditional "corner" and to hang above the cross-bed and down to side-bed level on each side of it. A "corner" was the arrangement of overlapping plates hung in the corner of the cabin side and table cupboard above the range. There were also some horse brasses and rosettes and a brass strip to edge the teapot shelf. The decorations were completed by a traditional cabin lamp made out of a brass piano candlestick holder in which was inserted an oil lamp with cut glass reservoir. The plates around my bed were a set depicting angels, which led to ribald comments from some of my friends.

On my first trip after I had put up all these decorations, I arrived at Sutton's after dark. Cabin doors open and lamplight shining on the brasses, I put New Hope round the turn, standing well back from the door hole as I did so. As I expected there were the usual few loiterers on the bridge and I got the hoped for compliment about my cabin. All I needed now was a better range and some crochet work. It was traditional to have at least a "ticket drawer piece" and maybe a length above the sidebed. I soon arranged for Violet Atkins to do me some crocheting (boatwomen used to do it while they were steering) but the range came a little later.

It may be as well to mention that some all male crews didn't decorate their cabins at all, but many did and went to great pains to make their boats as smart as possible. There was an element of competition in this. There was one period on the Northern Road when one boatman put on an extra tipcat. Others immediately did the same despite the nuisance of having to pull it up when going through short locks. This was followed by a craze for keeping Alsatian dogs. How they found the money to feed them I can't imagine and they took up a lot of cabin space.

Many boatmen liked pets, ranging from bantam hens and rabbits to the dreaded Teddy. Teddy was owned by Joe Skinner and had been trained to defend the Friendship and the valuable contents of her hold , mainly a collection of bikes, mangles etc and other useful items fished out of the cut, to the death. There was no way anybody could be invited aboard for a cup of tea until Teddy had been tied up in the hold. Bill Humphries had bantams, kept in the extreme front of the fore end where a space could be partitioned off without affecting the loading capacity. Grain for feeding them came from the sweepings off the British Waterways boats trading to Finney, Northampton and Wellingborough. Charlie Atkins had a tortoise which lived quite happily among the coal and Ray White went in for cats.

One thing about the Light job was that there was plenty of time for socialising. I found myself in the company of the Humphries quite a lot and would often butty them. If we stopped at Atherstone for the night we would all go to the pictures together and in the morning we would hang the two motors onto their butty for the lock free eleven mile pound to Sutton's. I would sometimes let their son Mike steer New Hope while I went back and steered their butty, an experience I rarely had the chance of enjoying. She was a smallish wooden boat and after the ex Grand Union butties I had been accustomed to she felt very light on the tiller.

More trips to the Light and then another load for the Conservancy completing their yearly order. Loading again at Newdigate I went to Hillmorton that night, then Fenny Compton, Banbury, Thrupp and Oxford, unloading the next day and getting back to the Pigeons. The Pigeons was a remote pub near Kirtlington. I had called in once or twice for a midday drink but this was the first time I had had the opportunity to spend the night there. As it relied on the canal trade, now practically nonexistent, it was almost empty and was soon to close. It was a pity it didn't survive into the pleasure craft age. On the way back I encountered Mike and Polly Rogers at Banbury. They gave me the range out of their boat Mabel , no longer required now that she was a hotel boat. It was a beautiful specimen, shining with polished steel and black-lead and I was very proud of it.

The two trips to Oxford, blessed as they were with fine weather, had been a delightful interlude but now it was back to short haul work. Two more trips to the Light and then a surprise order for J. Wright's (owners of the New World Cooker works) at Aston. This occasional but well paid job was worth 7s per ton plus a massive 4s 6d per ton for unloading. It had previously been done by "S.E."'s last pair of joey boatmen, Frankie Woodhouse and his son who had just left the job. Because of this I had been asked earlier to bring the last S. E. Barlow joeyboat back from the Light to Glascote dock. This was no problem even singlehanded. It didn't need to be steered and I worked the motor down the first five locks at Atherstone, tied it up and bowhauled the joey boat down, working it through the remaining two pairs of locks in a similar way.

With 20 tons 5cwt aboard the trip from Baddesley was fraught with difficulties. My log records "fast twice before Fazeley and three quarters of an hour below Common lock also below Dog, Minworth Green, Bottom Minworth, second bridge from top of Minworth, Erdington Hall and Trout Pool." It had taken 12 hours to cover 14 miles. I wasn't sure exactly where Wright's was located, on enquiry it turned out to be an inconspicuous door in a wall below the second from the bottom lock in the Aston flight. It was a grim place to spend the night and I wished I had stopped at Salford Bridge and gone there in the morning. I was well accustomed to mooring in the dingier parts of Birmingham but there was something about this place that made me feel uncomfortable. The coal had to be shovelled into a wheelbarrow and wheeled across the towpath, through the door and some distance inside. It took me a day and a half to get emptied singlehanded.

The long, hot days of summer had come to an end and I was thankful when cooler weather set in. Besides not being able to escape the blazing heat while confined to the footboard for hours round the long pounds, the undesirability of having the range alight in very hot weather made cooking very awkward as you had to stop in order to use the Primus because it was dangerous to leave it unattended.

I did one more trip to the Light and then, as it was getting towards the end of October and more boats were needed for the winter coal trade round Birmingham, I started doing some work for T.&S. Element, based at their wharf at Salford Bridge. I have already described this trade in detail in my earlier book, "No One". It consisted mainly of trips from Pooley to the GEC works at Witton, interspersed with loads from Walsall Wood Colliery to Wilmot, Breeden's at Tysely. If there was a freeze up I would work on the iceboat for which Element's provided horses and horsemen. I also did some work on Element's own horse-drawn open boats. I did one more trip to Wright's, this time being fortunate enough to get some assistance with unloading from three of my mates who worked for Element's, but I didn't much like the job and, as Joe Skinner expressed an interest in doing it, the matter was sorted to everyone's satisfaction.

CHAPTER TWO

BCN Backwoods

'Backwoods' was a phrase coined by Ray White to describe those parts of the BCN remote from the main line and, in those days, rarely visited by outsiders. A secret land of coal mines, brickworks and factories aptly described by his poetic words :
'Where hellbent boatmen work until they drop
With shaft and shovel, scrubbing brush and mop.'
The big advantage of working a cabin boat on the BCN was money. Carriage rates were far higher in this area than elsewhere, high enough to enable joey boatmen to have a modest house ashore and profitable for those who lived on board and thus avoided rent, rates, heating and various other expenses. This relative affluence had its price in the shape of an endless struggle with dirt, due to loading or unloading almost every day, and a great deal of wear and tear due to the bad condition of most of these cuts which the locals treated as rubbish dumps. Unless you were clever enough to avoid the hours in which they roamed, there were places where the local children would attack you with a range of missiles ranging from spittle to corrugated iron sheets. If they were close enough, a bucket of cold water would scatter them but they were usually too far away for effective retaliation. Add to this that most jobs required shovel work and it can be seen that the BCN was no place for those who preferred their boats to be smart and clean.

In my book "No. One" I recounted at some length the operations in which I participated, involving Element's work based at Salford Bridge wharf. Suffice it to say that this year again I worked mainly carrying coal from Pooley to the G.E.C. works at Witton and from Walsall Wood to Wilmott, Breeden's at Tyseley. Occasionally I would vary this with a trip from Pooley to Longford Light. It was possible to do three trips a week to the G.E.C. and I usually left Salford Bridge at 6 am on Monday, Wednesday and Friday, loading at Pooley the same day and returning to tie up at the Dog & Jacket pub at Bodymoor Heath. I was unloaded by lunchtime on Tuesdays, Thursdays and Saturdays which provided the opportunity to do some work on the weekday afternoons, for instance loading Element's boats at Saltley Sidings and perhaps towing a couple of boats round to the G.E.C., or I might take an empty boat up to the top of the 'New Uns' with another boatman and a horse and bring a loaded boat back.

Saturday afternoons usually meant a trip into the City, normally including going to the market where I could buy remaindered 78 rpm records to play on my recently acquired wind-up gramophone, perhaps a visit to New Street or Snow Hill stations for a bit of engine spotting, tea in the Lyons café in New Street followed by the pictures, returning to Salford bridge for a pint or two in the 'Muckman'. Occasionally I might catch the train to Wolverhampton and see who was tied up at the Top Lock. Sunday mornings were devoted to cleaning. If it was nice weather I might go to Sutton Park or the Lickeys, but having had plenty of exercise during the week I didn't really feel the need to go for long walks. Sunday evenings I sometimes went to New Street station with some of the other boat lads because we knew that on Sundays, girls would see their National Service boyfriends off on the train, then go in the buffet where they hoped to encounter someone to provide male companionship until the next weekend.

The Old Cut, as we called it, was in very poor condition and I regularly got stuck in one or other of the bridgeholes. I now carried a keb on board to rake out the obstructions, things like old bikes, prams and other unwanted junk and it was while I was engaged in this operation at Trout Pool bridge, the last one before Salford Bridge Junction, that a small, stocky figure appeared on the towpath and engaged me in conversation. This was my first encounter with Bobby, a retired boatman who lived in a converted butty moored in the Tame & Rea Drainage Board basin by the bridge. Bobby was a real character with a fund of stories. He had served in the First War on military craft in Mesopotamia, on the Tigris and Euphrates rivers. He had also been in jail and had had a varied waterway career including owning the *"Monarch"* which he used to tow Leonard Leigh's boats to the Weldless Steel Tube works at Wednesfield. Having made enough money to retire, he still liked the occasional business deal from which the other party was sure to come off worst. I was to come across him later on in my boating career.

It was possible to do two and a half trips in a week to Wilmott, Breeden at Tyseley and I preferred this route as being more convenient to work and having deeper water. However, you had to load your own boats at Walsall Wood colliery. This was not a problem but moving the empty rail wagons off the wharf and positioning the loaded ones aided only by a pinchbar, was difficult singlehanded. At Tyseley they liked to take all night to empty the boat, for some reason keeping it tipped up at an angle. Some sort of chemical was blown out of an extractor at the works that was damaging to your paintwork, perhaps it was fortunate that I never gave a thought as to what it might be doing to my lungs. People were, of course, accustomed to living in a smoky, dirty atmosphere in those days and you could have often shut your eyes and tell where you were on the cut simply by the smell. Going to Tyseley was handy as I could refuel there at the British Waterways depot.,With a 100 gallon fuel tank and a consumption of half a gallon an hour this didn't have to be done very often. Usually I would go from Salford Bridge or Tyseley, load at the colliery and spend the night at the 'Traveller' at Walsall Wood.

The 'Traveller's' stables were rarely empty and it was one of my favourite pubs, patronised by boatmen, busmen and miners and presided over by Tommy Fenn, a retired boxer. There was always a congenial, friendly atmosphere in the stone flagged bar and I was saddened when I heard the pub had closed and its adjoining row of cottages vacated in 1964 due to mining subsidence. The regular boatmen knew everyone who lived here, the Brookhouses, Dibbles, Grices and others and I wondered where they had all ended up. No doubt 'relocated' by a State intent on social engineering to some featureless housing estate or, even worse, to a tower block. How did they feel, deprived of their cosy community with their backyard gates opening onto the towpath and the boats passing by or tie-ing up?

When I worked for Elements I was in the habit of doing some work with their own horse drawn joey boats partly because it reduced the wear and tear on my own boat and partly just because I liked variety. This year there were alterations to some of the workings that gave rise to interesting opportunities. The Brownhills to Nechells Power Station working was a Leonard Leigh job. At one time his tug worked boats between Brownhills and the top of 'Mosses' (Rushall locks). Later the tug worked through, its four boats being bowhauled down the Ganzy and the New Thirteen, a spectacular operation in which a great deal of water was wasted. Each loaded boat would be flushed out of one lock by raising a top paddle and sucked into the lock below by raising half a bottom paddle, its course being directed by a boatman on the towpath using a long shaft. It was stopped in the lock by using the gate strap that at the same time shut the bottom gate with a bang. Coming up empty, the 'ellum would be removed and put in the hold, while the boat was bowhauled up the locks and stopped in each lock by drawing a top paddle. There was then no need to worry about the 'ellum being caught between the bottom gates as they slammed shut. The bang of slamming gates, the rattle of paddles as the pawls were knocked off the ratchets and they dropped with a thud, a turmoil of water everywhere, this was a part of canal life rarely seen by outsiders and difficult to imagine today!

This year it was decided to vary the operation and run the tug between Brownhills and the bottom of the Ganzy. From there Elements would work the boats to Nechells, one horse and two men to two boats. We would arrive at the bottom of Rushall to find the loaded boats waiting, cabins half full of water because, at Brownhills, the slack was loaded straight out of the washery and a lot had drained out by the time they reached Rushall, but this didn't worry us as we weren't going to need the cabin. The two boats, the forward one having had it's 'ellum removed and placed on top of the slack, were tied together, stem to stern so that the helmsman on the back boat could steer them as one unit, a procedure known as 'stemming'. We had a fire bucket, an old oil drum in which were punched holes. This was stood on an iron plate on the cabin top and contained a roaring fire. Setting off we soon reached Newtown Junction where the fastening between the two boats had to be loosened to get round the ninety degree turn. The horse line was dropped over the fore-stud of the first boat, placed round a pulley wheel and it was pulled round dragging its companion behind. The ropes were tightened up again and the pair of boats was 'stemmed' the two miles to the top of the 'New 'Uns' (Perry Bar Top Lock). We didn't carry any food on this job but refreshed ourselves in the coffee house at the top lock.

Going down the locks, we would work the boats down one at a time, stemming them for the quarter mile and mile pounds in the New Uns and between the bottom of Jill's and Nechells. I did quite a few trips on this job, usually with a young boatman named Albert Rooke who, in much later years, was to become well known as Birmingham's Harbourmaster.

We didn't escape the usual freeze up that winter and I had six days on the ice boat in early January, breaking ice from Salford bridge to Rushall, Icknield Port, Stone Cross and Longwood, bringing back a boat that had been frozen up at Stone Cross on the last day. There were still ice floes floating about in the cut when, one morning at the top of the New Uns, I was pushing a boat, that had been tied up there away from the bank so as to straighten it up to go in the top lock, when I slipped and fell in. It was frightening, I had visions of going underneath the boat or underneath a large piece of ice, but I came up with my head above water and hauled myself out. This wasn't my own boat so I hadn't got a change of clothes. All I could do was to steer and strap her down to Salford Bridge in my wet clothes which took an hour and a half. Fortunately she had a big fire in the cabin stove so I soon got fairly dry below the waist. At Salford Bridge I hastily changed and got on with the day's work.

Early in February I had a message from S. E. Barlow asking me if I would take a load to Banbury Dairy and tow back Bill Humphries who had broken down at Cropredy. I liked the Banbury run and jumped at the chance. George Element, who was short of boatmen, tried to persuade me not to go by forecasting that we hadn't yet seen the last of the frost. He was to be proved right! Loading 22 ½ tons of beans at Pooley on the 8th February I tied up at the top of Atherstone. The next day it started to freeze. I tied up on the turn by the railway bridge in the Braunston to Napton pound and next morning awoke to find half an inch of ice which I broke to the bottom of Napton where I tied up with Albert Beachy's two tar boats loaded for Banbury.

The bottom of Napton was a convenient place at which to be iced up, with water, shops and a pub all handy. That night we set out for the latter, Albert and I having to support his wife, Sue, who was a big lady, along the slippery street. We would have been sensible to have remained at Napton until the thaw, but on Monday the 13th a British Waterways iceboat turned up with a gang of men and we followed it to Fenny Compton. We had to tie up here as it was dark but the next day the iceboat decided not to break ice to the top of Claydon but instead to return to Napton. Had we been able to reach Claydon we knew that the disturbance of the water from working the locks would probably have weakened the ice as far as Cropredy where the influence of the river Cherwell which enters the canal there might have reduced the freezing down to Banbury.

We were at Fenny for fourteen days with nothing to do but keep the ice broken round the boats to prevent them being 'squeezed', and try to keep warm. Of course I had a whole boat-load of coal but it was what is known as peas, which describes the size of each particle, and would not burn without being mixed with something else to keep the fire open. Albert had a bit of lump coal and we sought out dead branches that we could saw up to mix with the peas. As the canal was frozen we could stand on the ice and reach the trees that overhung the outside of the canal at this point. They badly needed cutting back but instead of employing us to do this British Waterways sent a gang of men to take advantage of the access to them afforded by the ice. It was a thoroughly boring time and, although the George & Dragon pub was adjacent we were not being paid and were reluctant to spend more money than necessary.

Towards the end of this period I caught the bus to Cropredy where I found the Humphries'. They were quite happy as Bill and his son Mike had got a temporary job working on someone's lorry. I spent the night with them before returning to Finney from which we were finally released on the 29th getting to Cropredy that night. Here Bill hastily organised the sale of a quantity of coal to a neighbouring greenhouse owner, providing enough money for us to visit the pub. Bill and Mike came with me down to Banbury where we shovelled out our much needed cargo and returned to Cropredy, from where we made short work of towing Bill's boats back to Glascote. Because I worked as a single motor I never kept much ballast in for empty running. Pulling two boats was a different matter so we had to take up all *"New Hope's"* false floors and stack them up in the back end to get her stern down so as to get 'fan hold'. I didn't load again until March 5th so it had taken me a whole month to do one trip.

In spite of the Finney freeze up I had done quite well financially that winter and my thoughts turned to buying a butty. This was an idea I should have firmly put out of my mind. Owner boatmen should only have more than one boat if they have family to work them. There was no pool of labour queuing up for a boatman's job. However, I wasn't always as financially practical in my young days as I should have been. I wanted a butty and just hoped everything would work out. Hearing that the Mersey, Weaver & Ship Canal Carrying Company had just taken their *"Fitton"* out of service, I found out that she was for sale and went over to their dockyard at Middleport, Stoke on Trent, to have a look at her. She was an old boat but I couldn't see any obvious faults and she had been used for damageable cargos, so I thought I could get a few years out of her in the coal trade. Above all she was cheap, only £60.

Easter came and Brian Cusack, the younger brother of one of Element's boatmen took advantage of the school holidays to come with me to take *"New Hope"* round to the Potteries to collect her. On the way back we called in at Pooley and loaded both boats, putting about 21 tons on the butty. There were no problems with the journey, Brian was a strong lad and a competent boatman, but when we unloaded at the G.E.C. they complained that she was so narrow in the fore end that their grab would not work further forward than the mast. We had time before the end of the holiday to use her on a trip to Tyseley. It was a Saturday morning when we got back to the top of the New Uns so it was possible to borrow a horse to take her through the heavily locked part between there and Camp Hill. We walked the horse back from there before taking the pair to Tyseley. I left her there to be unloaded and worked both boats back to Salford Bridge singlehanded on the next trip. With 26 tons on we had no problems with *"Fitton"*. I steered her while we were behind the horse and she was a real pleasure to handle, one of those boats you could put through the eye of a needle.

The usual work pattern was resumed, not being broken until April 30th when Albert and I loaded an open boat at Saltley Sidings for Canning & Wildeblood on the Icknield Port Road Wharf loop line. All went well, we left our boat at Canning's and walked the horse back to Salford Bridge. Below the bottom of the '13' it lost its footing while going through a slippery bridgehole and fell in the cut. Such an occurrence was not uncommon and we attempted the usual method to get it out, that is by swimming it to a place where the water was shallow alongside the towpath, putting a strap under one foreleg and pulling it on to the towpath, then smacking its rump hard. Normally this would cause the horse to jump out. Unfortunately the horse wouldn't oblige despite repeated efforts. We couldn't let it stay in the cold water too long so had admit defeat and ring George Element. In those days there was a fire station on the towpath side in the Hospital pound and they put a sling under the horse and craned it out.

I had another chance to use *"Fitton"* , this time for a load of coal from Pooley to the Science Museum which was, in those days, situated in an old factory building just inside the Whitmore Arm in Farmer's Bridge locks. I towed her to Pooley single handed on a Friday and loaded her. On Friday evening a couple of my mates came down and we went as far as the Dog, working her in to the Wharf on Saturday morning. Sunday we borrowed a horse to take her up the locks. With three of us it didn't take long to shovel out her 23 tons of coal and we were back at base and in the Muckman by half past twelve.

In the spring and early summer of 1956 a variety of unusual traffic appeared at Salford Bridge. First of all some British Waterways Northern boats came down to load tubes at the Constructors factory at Tyburn Road for Liverpool via Weston Point. There was nowhere to wind there so one would have thought that they would have gone down facing the right way, loaded and proceeded to Weston via Fazeley, Fradley and the Potteries. Instead they worked empty to Constructors in reverse and came back through Salford Bridge. Next, a Whitsun stoppage on their normal route diverted a host of Northern boats from the Mersey ports to Birmingham and Wolverhampton via the Trent & Mersey and the Old Cut. These scoured out the channel considerably and also picked up a great deal of rubbish on their blades, so much so that my own operations were made much easier and I was bringing loads of up to 20 tons up to Witton for the rest of that season. Normally subcontractors were not needed by Elements after the end of April but that year I was still doing three trips a week at the end of June.

At the same time a stoppage in the '13' brought not only the diversion of the Clayton tar boat traffic from Windsor Street, Nechells and Solihull gasworks via the 'New 13' and West Bromwich Eight (Riders Green locks) but more Northern boats, this time loaded with rolls of steel. They told me they had loaded at Worcester and that the only crane in Birmingham of sufficient capacity to unload them was at Sampson Road wharf at the top of Camp Hill Locks. That was inconvenient enough but to make matters worse the stoppage caused them to take the long diversion via the Tame Valley canal. For me it was great to have cabin boats tying up for the night at Salford Bridge because I numbered many friends among the Northern boatmen.

One day towards the end of June as I was tied up at the wharf after emptying at Tyseley a strange boat appeared, painted an overall blue, with a single large 'T' bollard on her stern and identified only as "*Number 1*". At the helm was Jumbo Harris. He stopped for Marian to go to the shop and we had time to chat. Jumbo was in genial mood and well pleased with his boat and his present job. He told me that he had emptied steel at Camp Hill and was going empty boat to Brownhills to load coal for Worcester. This was the first I heard of this contract. Jumbo told me that it was being run by Fred Woollard, the British Waterways depot superintendent at Worcester and that there was a shortage of boats. Why didn't I give Fred (whom I knew) a ring?

Jumbo had hardly disappeared into the distance when I was on the phone, to be told that, yes, another boat was needed on the job and I could load at Brownhills for Worcester as soon as I liked. So it was farewell to Elements again. I liked George and my fellow boatmen at Elements but that sort of work, though profitable, was not my ideal of boating.

CHAPTER THREE

The Worcester Cut

I had never been to Brownhills or, to give it its correct name, Grove Colliery before. It is situated on the Cannock Extension Canal, five furlongs from its junction with the Wyrley & Essington at Pelsall. I arrived there in the evening to find a collection of joey boats waiting to load or be collected and the usual grimy jumble of pit buildings. Next morning the loaders called me under the loading chute first. As at Cannock (Anglesey) you had to remove your stands so that, when loaded, your top planks had to be arranged on top of the coal which was heaped high in the middle of the boat, the end of the back of the mast plank resting on the mast and the back end plank on the engine-hole roof. The coal was loaded straight out of the washery with no time to drain but, as with all washed coal, there was no dust. I was loaded, cleaned up and ready to go at 08:45.

Cup of tea on the cabin top, I engaged forward gear and gave her a good burst of speed; helm hard over to get round the junction with the main line. The Cannock Extension, known to us as the 'Edgford arm', was deep due to mining subsidence and it seemed no time at all before I was in the stop place at Pelsall where I turned right onto the Wyrley. There follows five miles of winding canal, rural at first but having canal side factories and houses as you approach Bloxwich with its two boatyards and the stop place where the toll clerk came out to gauge my boat, twenty two tons ten hundredweight.

Ticket safely in the ticket drawer, I put her round Birchills junction and, passing Birchills Power station with its many boats on the right, the top lock of the 'Walsall Eight' soon came in sight. The locks were not ready so I had to stop and fill the top lock, thereafter leaving the boat in the lock and filling the one below, carrying out this procedure until I got to the bottom of the flight. By then it was 12:30 so I made some sandwiches while I was in the bottom lock, ready to eat on the long pound to Great Bridge. It was a beautiful summer day and I felt blissfully happy as I steered along the six mile pound, brasses gleaming, white ash strips, cratch belt and strings scrubbed and everything as it should be. Just think....... I could go for a whole two days without having to get it all dirty again!

Below Walsall locks is the junction with the arm up into the town, destination of Franks' coal boats which were horse hauled by Peter Keay. The canal is lined with factories as far as Pleck where the gasworks had its tar collected by Thomas Clayton boats. The next place was Darlaston where, in a few years time, boats would load copper sludge for Liverpool. At Darlaston was the junction with the Bentley canal and some more factories. Richardson's works received creosote here from Oldbury in Clayton boats and there was a disused canal/railway interchange. Thereafter the canal ran through an area of long abandoned mine workings to Moxley where the old sand quarry, now owned by Ernie Thomas, was used as a tip for rubbish brought by horse boats.

Also at Moxley was Frost's galvanising works, to which Joshers had once brought cargos of zinc. Leaving the Bradley Locks branch on the right and the arm to the Patent Shaft Steel works on the left, you came to the Ocker Hill branch, up which was Masters' coal yard. Masters' had their own boats, also horse hauled by Peter Keay. A little further on come the disused Wednesbury railway interchange basin, followed by Wednesbury wharf. Hayward's tug still brought coal boats here and to the Patent Shaft. Ocker Hill power station followed, with its queue of waiting boats brought from Sandwell colliery by Ernie Thomas's horses.

In those days the Walsall canal was very much the province of horse haulage with Ernie Thomas, Peter Keay, Alan (Caggy) Stevens and T. & S. Element being represented.

Now we were approaching the bottom of the eight Riders Green locks, known to boatmen as West Bromwich Eight. At the junction with the Tame Valley Canal I could see a rubbish boat from Wilmot, Breeden's approaching in the distance. The Tipton Green & Toll End Communication (Tipton Old 'Uns) went off on our right, an alternative route that could be used if West Bromwich Eight was closed for repairs. The grimy chamber of the bottom lock loomed ahead, its approach flanked by two interchange basins and the Sheepwash arm, soon to be used by Willow Wren timber boats.

Riders Green locks were quick and easy to work and they were all ready for me thanks to meeting two loaded horse-boats. While rising up in the top lock I made a sandwich to eat on the long level into Birmingham. Thus fortified I relaxed for the two hour journey to the Bar Lock. By this time in the afternoon there was little trade moving and the only boats I met were a pair of British Waterways, empty out of Sherborne Street. But this part of the canal was never boring, you could see the red hot steel being rolled at the Roway iron works, and boats tucked away in basins and under side bridges waiting to be unloaded, as well as the trains on the Stour Valley railway line.

Worcester Bar lock, in those days, had four gates to allow for variations in water level but the fall was normally towards the Worcester cut. It was time to make another sandwich and put another mug of tea on the cabin top to keep me going until tying up time. It was about 5pm and I would normally have tied up here but everything was going well and I was in the mood to carry on. The water is deep as you leave the Bar lock but don't go too fast! The right angle Muck Turn was just ahead and needed precise positioning if you were not to catch your stern on the inside mud bank and end up hitting the outside wall. Fortunately I had been along here before and was wise to this hazard. It was fairly slow going out as far as Lifford because the canal, although originally intended for 14 ft beam craft, is quite narrow and the leaves from the thick tree growth alongside had caused some silting. The canal was eventually completed with narrow locks but a few wide barges had once worked on the summit.

The first convenient tying up place was Cadbury's wharf at Bournville but I decided not to join the four British Waterways boats tied up there waiting to load cocoa residue for Brentford but pressed on, past the Kings Norton Paper Works with it's tied up coal boats. Beyond Bournville the water was deeper and I was getting along quite nicely when the black mouth of Wast Hill tunnel loomed ahead. I had forgotten about this tunnel and had to stop to light my paraffin headlight and place it on the deck. I felt a bit uneasy, of course I had been through these long, wide gauge tunnels before but never by myself and never with only an oil lamp for illumination. The tunnel seemed creepy and a long way from anywhere or any one. Once I got inside I was alright, discovering that all I had to do was keep the glimmer of light at equal intensity on each of the side walls to steer straight. Having mastered that I opened up to full speed, tunnels like this were among the few parts of the canal deep enough to let rip with the throttle.

Without any warning I was suddenly enveloped in pitch darkness. The headlight had gone out! I hastily reversed to stop the boat and had to feel my way in the impenetrable gloom along the planks, round the cratch to the fore end and relight the lamp. It didn't go out again and I was soon back at full speed. Before long the patch of light at the other entrance could be seen and soon I was out in the open air again. But Wast Hill had another card to play. The cabin top, footboard and counter were covered with hundreds of pale, flea like insects. I realised that, not having a cutter on the exhaust pipe, I had blasted the tunnel's inhabitants from their resting place in the roof. I made sure I put an upturned shovel over the exhaust while going through tunnels until I got a pipe with a cutter. It was now about 8 pm so I stopped at Hopwood wharf, a very convenient tying up place. After I had mopped off, with special attention to removing insects, had a wash and a fry-up,

I had time to get a pint at the nearby pub. And so back to my cosy cabin and a last cigarette in bed with the firelight twinkling on my polished brasses. I fell asleep, feeling thoroughly satisfied with my day's work.

Next day I proceeded happily through the early morning sunshine, the savoury smell of frying bacon assailing my nostrils as it sizzled in its covered frying pan on the range. Is it my imagination or is it really true that bacon no longer smells the same as it did in those far off days? What could be better than a good fry up eaten off a plate on the cabin slide while steering? Once clear of Lifford the Worcester cut wound its way through deep country side, with plenty of turns to keep me occupied but nothing very difficult. The water was reasonably deep and I was making nearly three miles an hour which is good for a narrow canal. There are two more tunnels, both short, and on emerging from the last one I was at the top of Tardebigge locks, the canal maintenance yard on my right and in front a wide view over the Severn plain to the Malvern Hills.

Tardebigge top lock is very deep, with a drop of 14 feet and it is not possible to open the bottom gates and jump down onto the cabin top so as to drive the boat out. I solved this problem by drawing a bit of top paddle which got the boat moving. When she was half way out of the lock I dropped the paddle and stepped aboard below the lock. There is a half mile pound down to the Engine lock, so called because of the old pumping station adjacent. The remaining locks of the flight of thirty are all close together which makes single handed boating easy. The lock keepers were no longer available to help as things had been reorganised so that they spent their day with a work gang on different parts of the canal, returning only to put the locks right for the night. The locks were empty but all I had to do was put the boat in a lock, tie it down to the bottom gates, draw a little paddle and run down and fill the next lock, open its top gate and run back. By this time, the upper lock had emptied so I could open the gates, jump down and drive the boat out. It was all very quick and easy, a great change from the awkward locks on the Birmingham & Fazeley, not to mention being nice and clean and in very pleasant countryside. It took about three and a half hours to get down Tardebigge locks, had I had a bike I could have done them in three hours.

I hadn't seen any boats since passing the paper works but as I was working the top lock of the Stoke flight I saw some activity at the lock below. I passed the boat in the short pound between the locks; it was Jimmy Bradley with the *"Pike"* with a load of cases of tinned fruit for Tyseley. He told me that he hadn't met a boat since leaving Worcester so I should have the rest of the locks ready unless the lockkeepers had shut any top gates to prevent leakage. It was now about 1 pm and they wouldn't be back from their day's work until around 5 pm so I expected a good road. I went down the remaining Stoke locks in short order and out into the two mile Stoke pound. This stretch was very shallow, but not so bad that boats were likely to get stuck, and it was soft mud. Along here was the enormous salt and chemical works flanking both sides of the cut. This place had once provided a substantial trade with coal coming down and salt being sent to inland destinations and for export from Gloucester. The last trade had ended during the War when the consignee's depot at Holt Street, Birmingham had been destroyed by bombing. The six locks of Astwood flight were all ready, I was in luck this trip. It was quite common to have all 56 locks between Tardebigge and Worcester against you.

It was half past two when I cleared the bottom of Astwood and now I was able to relax for a while in the 'fiver', the five mile pound to Tibberton. This pound was noted for its high reed beds, known as 'segs', which lined it most of the way so that, when they were at their summer height, you couldn't see a great deal. It was rather a strange experience steering through this seg lined channel, akin to walking through a field of mature, head high maize. At the east end of Dennister (Dunhampstead) tunnel I met Lionel Tonks, with a Ballinger motorboat bound for Bournville with chocolate crumb from Frampton on the Gloucester & Berkeley Ship Canal. This was a shallow patch so he reversed back a few yards to the tunnel entrance to enable me to pass. I made sure the upturned shovel was over the exhaust, knowing that Dennister was full of spiders. Beyond the tunnel the Bristol to Birmingham main line railway comes close to the cut, affording a glimpse of impressive expresses or clanking goods trains, all steam hauled then of course.

Half past four saw me approaching the top of Parkers (Offerton locks). Great! The top gate was open and so were those in the remainder of the six locks, so I had cleared them by five pm. The next two locks were widely spaced with another long pound down to the top of the Bilford Four. The top gates at Bilford had been closed, but these didn't take long to work. The Lowesmoor pound below Bilford was very shallow in those days but I was carrying the water with me and went down without any trouble. All that remained were the Blockhouse and Kings Head locks, both very deep and awkward to work, before I emerged into the short stretch leading to Diglis Basin with the Porcelain works on the right. It was eight o'clock, I was too tired to want to walk round the town and settled for a visit to the fish and chip shop, which, together with a small grocers was, in those days, conveniently situated just over the bridge in Diglis Road.

I had cleared the planks and stands out of the way for unloading and was having breakfast when the two boat emptiers arrived at eight o'clock. While they got stuck into the coal I sauntered down to the British Waterways depot on the river where I was greeted warmly by the Superintendent, Fred Woollard and his assistant Sid Eades who explained the set-up to me. British Waterways South Western Division had disposed of the last of their narrow boats in 1949, since when the only regular traffic using the stretch of canal between Kings Norton and Worcester had been operated by Charlie Ballinger, an owner boatman based at Gloucester. The Royal Porcelain contract had been obtained through a commendable local initiative by these two men, both enthusiasts for canal carrying. They had negotiated with the Porcelain to remove the firm's rubbish and to carry the coal supplied through their factors the Cannock Chase Coal Company, a local Worcester firm. They had managed to obtain an ex- Grand Union motor boat that had been used as a fire fighting boat in Sharpness docks during the war, plus four of the Yarwood built British Railways boats made redundant in 1954. None of the station boats had cabins. Two were used for the rubbish contract and the other two on the coal job. Jumbo Harris had the motor and towed the station boats between Brownhills and Tardebigge with poor Marion standing out in the open to steer. Using the last canal company horse at Worcester, kept there only because it was needed twice a week to tow a tar boat between the gasworks and Diglis where the tar was pumped into a small river barge, Jumbo would leave his motor to be unloaded and take an empty boat up to Tardebigge with the horse returning with the loaded one. The two men who dealt with the rubbish boats and unloaded the coal were employed as casual labour. In those days no tax was deducted from British Waterways casual labour payments and quite a lot of men preferred to work on this basis.

Fred explained that they had difficulty in getting enough boats for the coal job. The North Western Division had lent them Jimmy Bradley with the *"Pike"*, but could only supply other boats when not required for their own traffic, so they would welcome a regular subcontractor. The rate offered was 12s per ton on the coal and there would be some back loading. As a matter of interest the factors were charged 22/6d per ton, out of which came 6s for tolls and 2/6d for unloading. After paying me they were left with 2/6d per ton which was a very fair arrangement.

Happy in having arranged a job which not only suited me very well but also looked like being long term employment I returned to the boat. It was still being unloaded so I made the men a cup of tea. Behind us, men were throwing 'seconds' into one of the rubbish boats. We would go through these but never succeeded in finding a whole piece of china, they had instructions to smash each piece and did so punctiliously. The next step was to do the shopping and visit the laundry. It paid to think carefully about shopping arrangements so as not to have to make unnecessary stops en route. There were then no laundrettes, the first one I came across was in 1960, so washing had either to go to a laundry, who took a week to return it, or you made an arrangement with some canal side lady to do it. Simple enough if you were on a regular run but not so easy if your route varied.

As for food, there was little in the way of convenience food, no fast food outlets apart from the chip shops and no pub grub as we know it today. There were plenty of shops in Sidbury, a street that crossed the canal at the Kings Head lock and was convenient to the 'Porcelain'. The thing to do was to stock up as much as possible before leaving Worcester. The round trip took four and a half days so it was necessary to buy bread and meat en route. At Birmingham I would use a corner shop grocer's two streets away from the Bar Lock. The shopkeeper had relatives who had worked on the cut and would always give regular customers a glass of port at Christmas. If I could I would pause in the last lock from the bottom of the Walsall flight where there was an excellent butchers close by in Wolverhampton Street.

We didn't have the variety of food that people nowadays enjoy but I am convinced that the meat and bacon then was of far tastier quality to that we get now and you got a lump of suet thrown in for nothing. As for refuelling the engine, I could do that at Wolverhampton or at Jimmy Yates's dock just before you got to Brownhills Colliery. I could do four round trips to Worcester on a tankful of 100 gallons.

Having sorted out these matters I returned to the boat which by now was nearly empty. It took about three and a half hours for two men to empty a boat here. When it was empty, having orders to return light to Brownhills, I replaced the planks, stands, beams and mast, all of which had to be moved out of the way while unloading, swept up the hold, mopped off thoroughly, winded in the basin and tied up outside the Anchor pub all ready to depart in the morning. It was lunch time by now and time for a pint. The next thing was to find the public baths which were some distance away in Sansome Walk. Every town had these baths in those days because of the large number of houses without bathrooms. Having luxuriated in hot, soapy water to my heart's content it was time for a walk round town, and a visit to the early house at the pictures. Worcester then boasted three cinemas. After tea in Lyon's, another long vanished institution, I found a milk bar in Angel Place. Milk bars, with their jukeboxes and opportunities for meeting the opposite sex, were the place to go for young people in those days and you did not see many in pubs, which, to them, were fairly boring places. I spent an hour in here, had a pleasant evening stroll back along the riverside to Diglis and so back to the boat.

It was a Friday when I started back, so, with no chance of loading until Monday, there was no need to rush. From Worcester to the top of Tardebigge is an easy run, with the opportunity to prepare vegetables, clean brasses and do other little jobs while the boat was rising in the lock chambers. It was easier going uphill, you usually found most of the locks empty and the bottom gates could be pushed open by the boat, no need to run ahead and open them. On the Saturday, seven hours boating brought me to Wolverhampton where I was able to spend the weekend with some of my old mates on the Northern boats.

When I got back to Worcester I was asked, while my boat was being unloaded, to go with Jumbo and fetch a loaded station boat, the "Ted", down from Tardebigge. We went up on the bus as he had taken the horse up with an empty boat the previous day. Coming down the locks, Jumbo steered and strapped while I 'drove and drawed' as the boating expression has it for driving the horse and drawing the paddles. Of course I also had to get the locks ready. We had no cabin and didn't bother to light the fire bucket as it was a hot day, contenting ourselves with a pint in the pub halfway down the locks in lieu of a cup of tea. The 'Halfway' was just a farmhouse kitchen a few yards from the 'halfway' lock of the Tardebigge flight. In the 'fiver' I got a chance to steer. It was the first time I had steered one of these station boats and you could control it with one finger, so light was the helm. But it only had 23 tons on, these boats had shallow holds and it was impossible to get a good load on them.

When we got to Parker's, the horse refused to go any further. It knew the cut as well as we did, and was accustomed to a day's work from Birmingham to Parker's. In the end we had to tie the boat up and ride the horse back to Worcester. We brought it up the next morning, having a job to get it to go past its accustomed stop at the gasworks. Really we should have tried blindfolding it at Parker's. I was glad to have had the opportunity to participate in the last regular horse-drawn traffic between Tardebigge and Worcester.

After another quick load of coal I had a back load of timber for Sampson Road, Birmingham, which involved going down the '13', and Ashtead locks and up Camp Hill locks to the Waterways depot there, returning empty to Brownhills via Camp Hill, Saltley, the New Thirteen and the Ganzy, which gave me chance to tie up at Salford Bridge and boast to my mates about my wonderful new job. I was advised of a stoppage on the Worcester cut so decided to go via the Stour cut. Knowing this to be shallow I put what I estimated was 18 tons on but I was booked 20 tons 10 cwt which I thought was an error in my favour. Loading in the morning I went down Wolverhampton locks the same day. This took two and a half hours as none of them were ready; in fact there was a conspicuous absence of Northern boats that day.

The first hundred yards of the Stour cut from Aldersley Junction was hard going, the cut being choked with mud but after that there was mostly an adequate depth of water. The locks on the Stour cut are awkward to work compared to the Worcester cut and there is a strange arrangement at the Bratch where there are three locks with the top gates of one and the bottom gates of the next separated by only a few feet of water. Half a mile below the Bratch is a road bridge and the Round Oak pub and here I got well and truly stuck in the bridge hole. By the time I had forced my way through it was teatime. There was no early finish in prospect that day because I knew that the Porcelain was about to start its two week annual holiday during which no boats would be unloaded. I decided to press on as far as I could, not knowing how long it would take to get to Stourport.

It was after eleven and pitch dark when I got to Wolverley lock and the boat jammed half way into the chamber. I had a look round and couldn't see any obstruction. Neither reversing nor drawing the bottom paddles and letting them down quickly, usually guaranteed to free a boat in this situation, had any effect. Feeling very cross I could do nothing except turn in, sleeping on the floor so as to ensure that I wouldn't oversleep in the morning. In those days the alarm clock didn't always wake me! It gets light early in July and at four o'clock it was light enough to see the problem. The iron guard that goes round the counter half way down and extends to the forward end of the engine hole had come loose sufficiently to catch the woodwork of the gate and had become firmly embedded therein. Drawing the bottom paddles had only made matters worse. This was caused by what is known as nail sickness, easily prevented by taking the guards off when the boat is docked, knocking plugs of new wood into the nail holes and nailing the guard back on again. Being short of money at the time I hadn't had this done when the boat was first docked and never thought about it subsequently.

Full speed astern, helped by pulling on a rope, did the trick this time, and having secured the guard again I went on my way getting to Worcester about one pm. All my effort was wasted as I soon discovered that the boat could not be unloaded until the end of the holiday. At least I had had the opportunity for a trip down the Stour Cut. I had only been down there once before, with a load of wool in 1950, and was never to disturb its waters again. Its local boatmen used to boast that it was the darkest cut in the Midlands and I never saw any reason to disagree with them.

I had to pump night and morning for the first couple of days waiting at Diglis as the washery water was still draining out of the coal. After I had painted everything that needed it there was nothing much else to do. The top pipe for the cabin chimney had burnt through so I had a new one, plus an exhaust pipe with cutter, made. There was a little workshop up the road that did this and made a very good job of it, charging much less than I had been charged at Barlow's. I fretted at the delay, being at that age when I liked to keep working and I didn't feel like a holiday myself. One morning there was a knock on the cabin side and I looked out to see Ray White standing on the towpath. He always liked to roam around when his boats were tied up. We caught the train at Foregate Street Station (little could I have imagined that forty years later I would be the Station Supervisor there) and got off at Stourbridge Junction, changing there to the push and pull shuttle to Stourbridge Town.

A short walk and we were at the terminal basin of the Stourbridge Arm. It was full of empty Western Region railway boats. I thought at first that this indicated the end of the Stourbridge to Swindon Iron Works traffic especially as I had not seen any signs of this work while going down the Stour Cut but it may have been that the works was closed for the annual holiday. Some sources state that the railway boats to Swindon finished in 1958, two years later.

Crossing the road we entered the yard behind the canal warehouse and then had to walk through an ironworks to gain the towpath. Neither of us had visited this part of the canal system before and it was all new and interesting despite the absence of any traffic. After a mile we came to the main line at Wordsley Junction and started to climb a flight of locks known as The Sixteen surrounded by heavy industry all the way. At the top of the flight is

Leys Junction where the main line takes a right angled turn and the Fens Branch continues straight on. We walked up the Fens Branch coming, after a few yards, to a side bridge from which we were surprised to see a wharf and shed with boats being unloaded into railway wagons. This was the British Railways (WR) Bromley Basin. Readers may be surprised that we didn't know it existed but at that time it was quite usual for boatmen to be completely ignorant of parts of the canal away from their own trading routes. Of course we had to have a closer look and were intrigued to discover that the boats contained firebricks and that they were being unloaded by women who regarded our appearance on the towpath as an opportunity for an exchange of suggestive remarks, the more so as they were safely separated from us by the width of the canal.

But there was more. Beyond the wharf stood an unusual structure which, on closer inspection turned out to be a guillotine lock. Sadly we were not equipped with cameras and it is only recently that I have seen a good photo of this lock. Running the verbal gauntlet of the brick handling ladies we retraced our steps and followed the main line towards Dudley. At Black Delph we found several firebrick works with boats being loaded. They were towed to Bromley with one horse to two boats. We climbed up the impressive flight of locks, known as The Nine although long since rebuilt with only eight deep locks, and wended our way through the depths of Round Oak ironworks to Parkhead. Here we investigated the remains of the Pensnett Canal, a waterway which had been in use only five years previously and found our way over the top of Dudley tunnel to Dudley station just in time to catch the train to Birmingham from where Ray returned to Coventry and I caught a train back to Worcester.

After the end of the holiday "*New Hope*" unloaded her coal and went down and loaded 16 tons of timber from a river barge for Jones's yard at Wolverhampton. To get a full load of timber on it was necessary to move the mast and secure it up against the cratch so as to give more hold space. The sawn deals, all of different lengths, were then laid in place piece by piece so there were as few gaps as possible. Despite careful loading it was only possible to get 14 to 16 tons on board but timber carried a higher rate of pay per ton. I received £11 4s for this load which was good considering that the light load meant it was possible to get along faster. The trip to Wolverhampton was sheer joy with none of the usual slow going through the shallow stretch between Kings Norton and Tipton. The timber yard was situated just inside the arm by Wolverhampton Power Station.

Another load of coal was followed by another load of timber to Wolverhampton. On arriving back at Worcester I was given a load of steel coils to Stourport. Around this time this steel was being imported for the Austin Motor Works at Longbridge (Birmingham), the ships arriving at Avonmouth and the steel being barged to Worcester. The coils had to be protected from the weather and, having run short of covered space at Worcester, it was necessary to send some to Stourport for storage. These coils were heavy, weighing about six tons each and I loaded three, making about 18 tons, not wishing to work the river with 24 tons without side cloths. 3s 6d per ton for a two and a half hours trip in nice deep water suited me fine!

Back at Worcester a cargo of aluminium was available for Sherborne Street, Birmingham, 23 tons at 10s per ton and for the next month I was going hell for leather with aluminium up and coal down, seven cargoes in 31 days.

Fred Woollard always liked to try new things. One of his ideas was to experiment with the use of an auger for unloading coal at the Porcelain. He borrowed one from somewhere, we couldn't rig it up properly, to get the best work out of one you need to suspend it from a gantry in such a way that it can be moved up and down and from side to side. However, we propped it up with one end on top of a ruck of coal in the boat and switched it on. The results were startling. In no time it had dug itself down to the floorboards. Ideally we should now have been able to move it to get into the corners of the room we were working in. As it was we had to shovel the rest of the coal to it before starting on the next room. Even this makeshift arrangement saved a lot of time and, more important, the effort of throwing coal onto an already high mountain of the stuff.

Alas! Like so many improvements to boat emptying that could have been made at little cost , this one fell foul of obstruction by the labour force. The two casual workers recognised the auger as a threat to their earnings and threatened to stop unloading the pottery scrap boats if its use was continued. It would have cut the cost of unloading boats by about 1s 6d per ton.

This job was boater's heaven as far as I was concerned. The route was interesting with the contrast between the mining scenery on the Chase, the heavy industry between Walsall and Birmingham, and the deep countryside beyond Kings Norton. The cut was easy to work with handy locks and no obstacles in the shape of drawbridges or swingbridges and there was an adequate depth of water. I enjoyed the long Wast Hill tunnel, belting through it at full throttle and passing the time in its gloomy depths by singing at the top of my voice. I was also earning plenty of money. I didn't see why I couldn't go on doing this job for years.

In October I decided that the engine had better have its annual overhaul at Ted Jones' dock. Having acquired a set of side clothes from Bobby Gopshill I was going to fit those at the same time, intending also to order a set of top cloths so that I could accept some of the cargoes of tinned foodstuffs often available as a back load from Worcester. I agreed this with Fred Woollard, I did not expect to be away more than a few days and the wharf at the Porcelain was piled high with coal.

On examination it was discovered that the cylinders needed new liners and there was some delay in obtaining these from Ruston's factory. While I was at Glascote I had a message to say that there was no longer any work available for me on the Worcester run. Having been promised a regular job I couldn't understand this and went to see the District Traffic Officer at Bridge Street, Birmingham, Mr Oxley who was an old B.C.N. man. His excuse was that British Waterways wanted the work for its North Western boats but that I had no cause for complaint as he had found another job for me. This job turned out to be a return to working for Element's on the Pooley Hall to Witton run.

Suddenly light dawned on me. The big B.C.N. carriers and British Waterways had a very cosy relationship and obviously, with winter about to start and a severe shortage of boatmen, Elements had asked Oxley to stop me on the Worcester cut so I would have to return to working for him. I had no objection to working for Element's, in fact I would have like to have helped him out and the job was well paid, but I did object to working on the Old Cut with its constant groundings and propeller fouling and excessive wear and tear on the boat so I told Oxley, in no uncertain terms, what he could do with his crafty arrangement.

As it happened, Oxley's decision was not, in the end, a good one for the Worcester Cut. The Suez Crisis was about to break. It will be remembered that an abortive attempt to prevent Egypt from nationalising the Suez Canal resulted in the blockage of that waterway and this country having to resort to fuel rationing. A great deal of traffic was diverted onto the inland waterways and the North Western Division found itself overwhelmed with work .Among their new cargoes were glass and wire but old Shroppy boatmen will remember in particular the barrels of lubricating oil carried from Ellesmere Port (loaded at Chester) to Wolverhampton, on which job they could work hell for leather. As the N.W. Division received no tolls from the Worcester job they gave priority to their own work and it became difficult to keep up the coal supply to the Porcelain.

But this was all in the future and, in the mean time, I had no trouble arranging to work for S.E. Barlow on the Longford Light job. It wasn't very well paid but would do for the time being. George Element, having failed to persuade me to work for him over the phone came down to Glascote. I can remember the scene to this day. Ted's yard was approached through a field full of cows. George parked his car at Ted's gate and was using his best powers of persuasion on me while at the same time trying to stop a number of curious cows from scratching his shiny new vehicle. Eventually I agreed to do one trial trip to Witton but made it clear that if I had any trouble I would not take on the job for the winter.

I wasn't at all surprised that my trip to Witton with a mere 17 tons 5cwt revealed that there had been no improvement to the cut since I had last worked up there. It just was not in a fit state for loaded motor boats. I settled down to work to the Light, a nice easy going job with no navigational problems. I was better off than I expected as the rate had been increased to 4s 6d per ton and I found that I could get upwards of 24 tons on giving me around £11 per week. Sometimes I would end up with 25 tons aboard but, apart from the general slow going, I never had any trouble. Around this time I had to obtain an exemption from diesel oil rationing from the Post Office at Atherstone. I think it was at about the same time when I bought my first Premium Bond.

I hadn't done many trips to the Light before I started to get the occasional order for Rugby Co-op, from Griff, very profitable at 7s 5d per ton.

The beginning of 1957 coincided with the retirement of Joe Skinner from the Banbury Dairy job and I took it over. Joe and Rose gave me the address of a man who used to help them shovel the coal out at the Dairy which was useful as I was not over fond of shovel work if it could be avoided. I loaded for the first time for the Dairy at Griff on the 2nd of January, with a big load of 24 tons 2cwt and had a pleasant trip to Banbury. The rate was 13s 9d so this gave me £15 7s 3d. The Skinners unloader at Banbury was a man called Paddy Fury. He slept rough by choice and could be contacted via his usual pub. Paddy was a really nice guy and handled a shovel like a teaspoon. He had been in submarines in the war and, after discharge, had discovered his wife had been having an affair in his absence. He left home and, as a matter of principle, refused to pay her any maintenance. This meant that every six months he was arrested and had to spend a couple of weeks in prison. Having someone to help unload was a great help, we could do it in three hours and after cleaning up I would usually spend the rest of the day at Banbury.

The Dairy only required three loads a month. Coming back empty I would often bypass the Boat Control Office while it was closed and go straight down to Pooley and load for the light, rather to the annoyance of Mr Shaw. "I might want to send you somewhere else" he would say, to which the obvious answer was "Such as where?" Life settled into a happy routine, a trip to the Dairy followed by two to the Light. The Skinners were still working to the Light and to Rugby, on one occasion I followed them out of Pooley with a greater tonnage on my motor than they had on their horse boat.

CHAPTER 4

Down the Junction

Once again I was convinced that I was settled for a long period in a congenial job, and once again I was to be disappointed. At the end of January 1957, S.E. Barlow sold out to the Samuel Barlow Coal Co. and out of the blue I found myself with an order for the Co-op at Leighton Buzzard. The idea of going down the 'Junction' with a single motor had never occurred to me, I suppose I had some vague idea that single boats would not be welcomed down there because of the waste of water with one boat in a wide lock. Anyway I loaded at Newdigate and found I could manage the 'Junction' reasonably well. Singlehanded motors were at a disadvantage as the locks were by no means convenient for this kind of working. Two-handed pairs could travel long distances breasted up, for instance through the flights of locks, and thus the pair could be worked as a two-handed single unit in these circumstances. Singlehanded, if the locks were ready you had a fast journey. If not, it was painfully slow because most of the Junction locks were so far apart that you had to stop above or below each one to fill or empty it.

Unloading at Leighton was by shovel and barrow across the towpath and I had only got a few tons out when who should appear but Ray White with "*Tiger*" and "*Jane*" travelling empty to the coalfield. They tied up and Ray and Muriel helped me to unload my cargo. It was quite a common practice when you came across one of your mates unloading with a shovel to stop and help out. At Leighton I met Mr Keef of the Wyvern Shipping Company, who revealed that this was their traffic, subcontracted to Barlows, and kindly told me the rate he paid them.

When I got back to Braunston I discovered that there was an enormous difference between what they paid me and what they were being paid. They got 17s 6d per ton and I got 12s 6d. As I have mentioned it was normal for the main contractor to take no more than 10% and in many cases a much lower commission. I considered I should have been paid 15s 9d per ton and thereafter my feelings toward Barlows were not of the warmest.

My regular trips to Banbury ceased and I did six trips to the Light before getting another load for the Dairy. I loaded 25 tons 8 cwt and sometimes nowadays I can hardly believe the heavy loads I used to take over this route. There followed two more trips to the Light, a Banbury and a Rugby. On this trip to Rugby I towed Skinner's "Friendship", I had loaded at Griff and they at Newdigate.

My discontent with Barlows had led me to approach the Willow Wren Canal Carrying Company. They had a contract from Cannock to Nestles at Hayes and I reasoned that I would have the advantage of single locks as far as Camp Hill on that job and the rate, at 23s per ton was good enough to compensate for the awkward work with a single handed boat down the Junction. It was as well I had made this arrangement as the job to Longford Light finished altogether in April. One result of this was the closure of refuelling facilities at the Greyhound. The boat docks at Polesworth and Glascote had already closed.

I didn't do very well on this trip, being caught in a Bank Holiday stoppage at Braunston and again held up when a pair of Waterways boats got the stem of one of their boats under the top gate of the lock below Hunton Bridge and lifted it out. This could happen easily if you were careless. On stopping above an empty lock to fill it, the tremendous suction caused by having all the top paddles open would cause a drop in the water level immediately above the lock. If you allowed your boat to get right up against the gate the fore end would catch under the heavy beam across the top of the gate and lift the gate up when, as the lock filled, the water regained its normal level. I did better coming back, doing Hayes to Cowroast in eleven and a quarter hours. I had the method of working single handed on this canal well sussed out, the only problem I couldn't resolve was the banging about the boat got when empty in uphill locks. It was the custom to step ashore with a strap attached to the anser pin to stop the boat. When the paddles were drawn there was nothing to stop it swinging across and clouting the opposite wall with the fore end. On reflection, I think I should have tried putting the strap on the back-end rail which is nearer to the middle of the boat. You had to do this anyway in the 'New' locks between Napton and Birmingham because of the location of the uphill strapping post.

I avoided the New locks on the way back by going empty via Fradley and on arrival in the Four Mile pound I was amazed to see a steam dredger at work, with young Tommy Platt on board, in spite of the fact that the G.E.C. coal contract had been transferred to Walsall Wood in April.

I had called at Barlows to refuel on the way back and fell in with David Campbell who had replaced John Knill as Boat Manager. A man and wife were there applying for a pair of boats. He told them he hadn't got a pair vacant at the moment and referred them to me. I had the "*Fitton*" still tied up at Salford Bridge, and, now I had a job suitable for a pair, this was the chance to get some work out of her. David boasted to me afterwards that he knew this boatman had an unreliable reputation and thought it would be funny to palm him off on me. I was not amused at his irresponsible behaviour.

We loaded at Cannock and found, as I expected, that "*Fitton*" was leaking. She had not had a load in for a long time and her timbers had dried out. I told my mate, whose name was Bill, to let her drag along the side in those parts of the cut where the banks were being continually built up with clay to counteract subsidence. The idea, commonly used to deal with leaky boats, was that the clay would block some of the leaks until the planks took up. The leaking improved but we still had to pump her regularly. We had put 26 tons on "*Fitton*". She never loaded more than 20 tons for Mersey, Weavers and additionally she liked to have the middle kept light with most of the weight in the two ends which we couldn't do when putting in a full load.

We tied at the bottom of the Ganzy that night and, after a pumping session, went to bed. When I looked out next morning I could see that "Fitton" was very deep in the water. Before I could wake up my crew she gave a lurch and dropped a couple of inches, putting the middle of the port side gunwhale under water. To see the look on the faces of my mates as they scrambled out of the cabin would have been funny in more propitious circumstances. I was annoyed but not worried; raising sunken boats was part of everyday life on the B.C.N. I rang up British Waterways who sent a gang of men. Putting an empty boat on each side of "Fitton", they manoeuvred a couple of wire cables underneath, connected them to jacks and raised here the couple of inches necessary to get the gunwhale above water. A motor pump removed most of the water and our hand pump did the rest.

It was summer and long hours of daylight and we made good time down to the 'Cocoa'. Bill knew how to boat but his wife had to be watched like a hawk in case she let the butty drop back in the wide locks and catch the helm on the bottom gates. When we got out of Camp Hill, I let Bill have the motor for a bit so I could have a go steering "Fitton". She had very fine lines and swam like a fish, requiring only a very light touch on the tiller. Quite different from my previous experiences with ex Grand Union butties like "Uranus", "Raven" and "Warwick". That was the only time I steered her, thereafter I stayed on the motor and let my mates get on with the butty and the lockwheeling.

I had thought Braunston and Blisworth tunnels might present a problem to my crew but we sailed through in fine style. I liked to drive hard in the downhill locks and, not trusting Bill's missus to use the downhill strap, I stopped the boat with a strap on the fore end. I could stop the motor, get off and start the top gate closing, then jump onto "Fitton's" fore end as she swept by. With Bill lock wheeling we made good time. Sometimes after a good day and a nice big supper, I would think back to my early days as a mate on the Northern Road, the food rationing, lack of money and struggle to master proper boating techniques.

After unloading at the 'Cocoa' we had orders to go to Brentford for a load of timber to Finney. It was a light cargo so we had no problems with leaks. *"Fitton"* was a bit of a watercress bed, in boatman's parlance and we had had to pump her every evening on the way down and *"New Hope"* had always made a drop of water, not very much, when loaded. At Finney we were very fortunate in getting orders to go empty to the coalfields for Slough, only a day's empty boating. We loaded at Newdigate with house coal for a merchant at the end of the Slough arm. For the first time in my experience of the house coal trade I encountered modern unloading facilities. A mobile grab picked up the coal and deposited it in two mobile hoppers, designed to bag and weigh the coal before dropping the bag on the deck of a delivery lorry. After a night in the lay-bye at Bull's Bridge in the company of Charlie and Violet Atkins, it was down to Brentford again for a load of timber for Great Bridge, buttying the Barrett family all the way to Cox's timber yard up the Sheepwash Arm. There were a lot of boats waiting to unload here so we had several days rest before going once more to Cannock for Hayes Cocoa.

So far so good! We had made some quick and profitable trips and I was enjoying three handed boating down the Junction. *"Fitton"* was earning £32 for every trip to the Cocoa and I was paying £6 per trip, plus food, to the crew. This was about the same as the British Waterways rate for a single boat. Moreover we got along much faster than I could have done when singlehanded with *"New Hope"* so extra earnings to the motor were a bonus. Moreover my crew had given me no trouble at all so far. When we got tied up at Hayes I gave Bill some money and asked him to get the shopping while I emptied the boats. When they were unloaded and he still hadn't returned I began to wonder where he was. Night came and no Bill. In fact I wasn't to see him again for three years.

This left me with a pair of boats and Bill's wife. We set off empty back to Braunston where I intended to leave *"Fitton"* and send the good lady home to the salubrious shores of Spon Lane, from where the couple came, on the train. The trip wasn't too bad; being empty we could go abreast a lot of the way. It took three days to get back to Braunston, the only incident being in the Jackdaw pound. It was very windy and I couldn't get a start out of the lock, bearing in mind that you went down this pound singled up and I needed to slow right down to pick up the cross straps. My fore end kept blowing ashore before I could get fanhold.

The reason for this was lack of ballast. When single motoring I had avoided putting much ballast in *"New Hope"* so as to get as many tons on her as possible. I could manage her without ballast as a single boat but she needed it when towing. Someone had told me that the thing to do in such circumstances was to tow on a longish bit of line so that you didn't need to nearly stop when picking up the tow. This worked but the expression on the faces of the crew of a Waterways pair who met us going along like this had to be seen to be believed.

I left *"Fitton"* at Braunston, going empty to Cannock. Nowadays you often hear complaints about the heaviness of the new locks after Napton but I thought they had advantages. Most of them were close together in flights so you could leave your boat in one lock and go and prepare the next. As for the 21 at Hatton, I have once gone up them in as little as two hours single handed. They were, however, all ready for me. I spent the first night at Long Itchingdon in the company of Sam and Sue Beachy with their tar boats. In the pub I was introduced to Sam's mother who regaled me with an account of how her husband had once sold her for 30s. He bought her back the next morning.

Being empty I decided to go via the northern part of the Stratford Cut which saves a lot of lockage. Back in 1952, British Waterways had spent a lot of money dredging this but I found it slow going and would not have like to attempt it with even a light load. Also it was encumbered with swing bridges and drawbridges, all heavy and awkward to work. One I managed to open and couldn't get shut afterwards and I was pursued for a quarter of a mile along the outside bank by an irate gentlemen demanding to know why I hadn't closed the b...... bridge. I spent the night at Shirley and the next at Wolverhampton, pausing briefly at the Bar Lock to buy a new primus stove. They cost £2 10s at the time. The trip south from Cannock was slow, taking six days. How I missed the exhilaration of fast working with a three handed pair.

Loading timber again at Brentford, I was surprised and pleased to see a single motor arrive, captained by my old friend Jim. On finishing his National Service he had been unfortunate enough to be called up into the Reserve at the time of the Cyprus conflict and I hadn't seen him since 1951, although we had kept in touch. The North Western Division had bought the *"Daffodil"*, a wooden, big engine Josher, and he had been sent down to Bulls Bridge to bring it back. With Jim was young George Brooks. While I painstakingly selected pieces of timber of the right length in order to get a good load on, Jim threw his in anyhow and ended up with about five tons as against my fifteen. Of course he got paid a twenty ton minimum whereas I was only paid for what I actually carried! *"Daffodil"* buttied me to Great Bridge, as she was more lightly loaded and had a more powerful engine we towed on a line in the long pounds. It was a pleasant trip, with good company and the usual leg pulling that goes on when boatmen get together, especially when you have caught one of your mates being invited into a young lady's cabin with instructions to "Come and keep me warm."

We spent two days at Great Bridge in the company of the Barratt's and a pair of British Waterway's boats before I got orders for Newdigate for Banbury. On the way I spent three days at Salford Bridge Wharf because of a stoppage at Curdworth. I was chatting to George Element and got brought up to date on the traffic position there. The coal allocation to the G.E.C. had been changed from Pooley to Walsall Wood and that for Wilmot, Breeden from Walsall Wood to Brownhills. It occurred to me that Brownhills to Wilmot's (Tyseley) might be a convenient job for the winter and George said he would get in touch in October.

There had been other alterations, for instance Constructor's Ltd at Tyburn Road was now served from Brownhills instead of Saltley Sidings and the Suez crisis had brought a new traffic of coal to the basin above the ninth lock at Perry Bar. This did not survive the Suez crisis as it had to be carted to its final destination, one of Lucas's factories.

I had been suffering for a while with leaks in the cabin roof and, not having had a docking since 1954, decided to have the boat caulked, tarred, repainted and one or two other minor jobs done. The order was best house coal for Palmer's, a coal merchant at Cherwell Wharf, Banbury at 13s 3d per ton, considerably more than Barlow's had paid me for Banbury Dairy. Unloading was by shovel and barrow. As I had some help it only took about eight hours. I arranged with George Tooley to dock the boat and then went looking for a temporary job ashore while it was being done. Before I had found one I had a visit from David Campbell who asked me if I would like to take a party of Scouts for a camping trip on a pair of his boats. "*Mabel*" was at the dock and Polly Rogers kindly took me over to Braunston in her van which was handy as I needed to take some bedding and cooking equipment.

On arrival at Braunston I was given the "*Franklyn*". She was the former Josher "*Vanguard*", renamed when she had been bought by S.E. Barlow. I can't remember the name of the butty. I made myself comfortable in the motor's cabin, started her 15hp Bolinder to make sure it was running properly and spent a lazy four days awaiting the arrival of the Scouts who were from Aylesbury.

I had put most of the sidecloths up and two of the top cloths on each boat so that they would have a covered area. The Patrol Leaders all slept in the butty's cabin and the two Scoutmasters had a tent ashore. We set off after lunch heading for the Cape, doing only short days of course. I shared in the Scouts meals which saved me cooking. The weather was sunny and we had an enjoyable trip, usually tying above a lock which, when filled, made a convenient swimming pool. All the usual Scout camp activities took place including impromptu games of football. Invited to join in, I was surprised to find myself out of breath after a few minutes... however did I manage all that lock work and shovelling? The answer is that it is a different form of exercise. As a schoolboy I had been a keen Scout and the annual camp was the highlight of my year so I felt quite at home and was able to give some tuition on knots and splices.

The boys soon learned how to work the locks. I had made sure David Campbell had provided them with windlasses as I didn't want mine dropped in the cut, but in the event they didn't lose any. Otherwise all they had to do was to steer the butty straight when entering the locks and I stopped it with the stern string on the motor's dolly. It might have been fun to teach them how to use an uphill strap but I hadn't brought one with me.

We went as far as the top of Cape Locks before winding and retracing our steps back past Braunston. By this time one or two of the more senior Scouts would come and keep me company on the motor while we were going along and I let them have a go at the tiller where the cut was straight. Everyone was suitably impressed by Braunston tunnel, especially as we met two pairs inside. Turning off at Norton Junction we headed for Crick, giving them an opportunity to bowhaul up Watford locks. After a couple of days at Crich it was back to Braunston. Everyone was pleased with their holiday and I had several offers to come and crew for me during the next school holidays. What made the trip even more enjoyable for me was to get my hands on a Bolinder. I have always had a definite preference for these engines.

I had taken a fancy to *"Franklyn"*, and knowing that she was surplus to Barlow's requirements, I asked if I could buy her. I was surprised to get a refusal. "We don't want her getting into Morton's hands" was the reason. An offer to hire her while my boat was on the dock was refused for the same reason. I had found Willow Wren a good firm to work for, with good rates and prompt cash payment, but it has to be admitted that Leslie Morton was a bit of a pirate and had no qualms about cutting the price on contracts and attracting other firms' boatmen by paying higher wages. Barlow's did not take this kindly, especially as Willow Wren's backers put up with them making a loss every year, whereas other carriers had to stay in profit. I then suggested that if they sold it to me I would subcontract for them, but having lost the Longford Light job, they were short of work. I knew they still had the Sandford mill contract, now sent by road, and suggested it could be put back on the cut and I would do it. David actually rang Mr Sands about this but he wouldn't hear of it. Which reminds me of one of Ray White's *bon mots* "The future of Barlow's is based upon shifting Sands."

When you are embroiled in the hurly- burly of active boating it is difficult to see the wood for the trees. I was not particularly worried by the fact that *"New Hope"* was now 22 years old but it crossed my mind that my Ruston engine had come from Barlow's and they had a reason for taking it out of *Cairo* after only a few years of service. I believe it had had two crankshaft replacements. It was not a very powerful engine and had had to be thrashed up and down the Junction towing a butty whereas I had rarely used it for towing and never driven it hard. On most of the narrow canals you could only use a small throttle opening anyway because of the lack of depth. I probably had not given it much wear but couldn't be sure when expensive repairs might be necessary. So my desire for a change of boat, though driven purely by my desire to have a different boat to play with, had a subconscious rationale.

This might also have been a good time to think about the traffic situation. I didn't know what was in the minds of the Coal Board, the Central Electricity Generating Board or British Waterways but the loss of the coal traffic to Longford Light should have sounded alarm bells. This traffic had been very useful to me in the past and the fact that I had always been able to get a load for there would be missed. Another thing was the declining number of boatyards, both S.E. Barlow's and Lees & Atkins having recently closed down. Had I had this information I would have known that within ten years the amount of canal traffic left would be negligible.

Another thing that I had not taken on board was that the British Waterways South Eastern Division fleet was slowly becoming smaller and that was the place to enquire about buying a boat. I didn't have any useful contacts there but I could have asked Leslie Morton's advice.

As for Barlow's, David told me many years later that he had been given the job to manage the running down of the fleet during the period of transfer of traffic to lorries. Even then they hadn't a great deal of canal work left, having lost the Light (to their own lorries) and Hayes Cocoa (which they shared with British Waterways) to Willow Wren. They subsequently got some of the latter back. Apart from this they had only Kearley &Tongue's at Southall and Frogmore and Home Park paper mills. They did some work for British Waterways but had lost a lot of their best Captains to Willow Wren.

Returning to Braunston I found George Tooley hadn't made a start on my boat nor could he say when he would. Reluctantly I decided to take it to Braunston, where they made the usual good job of docking, curing the cabin leaks by sheathing the top with marine grade plywood, something they did to their own boats as each went on the dock. Another problem, not quite solved as I found out later, was a small crack in the counter block between the hole bored for the rudder post and the cabin. This only leaked when putting the helm over when loaded as the wash was then forced up the hole. The solution was a wide rubber ring put round the rudder post which would be forced up against the bottom of the counter by the force of the wash and prevent the water going up the hole. It did, in fact, alleviate the problem but sooner or later I thought a new counter block would be needed.

"New Hope" looked good when she came off the dock. I had changed the colour of the cabin side surrounds from oak grain to green with a yellow line between them and the red of the main panel. The top bends followed the Josher style of red and blue sepa-

rate by a yellow disc with a yellow crescent at the rearmost end. This was supposed to represent night and day and sun and moon. I didn't go in for fancy decoration (and there were other boatmen who preferred plain colours on the cabin side and fore end) but had the usual roses and castles on the cabin doors.

I went to check on "*Fitton*" who I had left moored to the bank below the bottom lock. She was full of water and I had to borrow a motor pump to get her dry. British Waterways wanted her moved and I was pondering what to do with her when a chap came along and offered to take her off my hands and break her up for the scrap value of the ironwork. She was old and leaky and I had no crew for her so I was glad to take up the offer. She had only cost me £60, I had more than recovered that and had a lot of enjoyment from her into the bargain. I was sad to see her go, she was a pretty boat and a fast swimmer but she had been lightly built, "for a short life and a merry one" as one boatman put it. He also described her as "laying well under the wind". Sometimes I daydream of a boatman's heaven where myself and a couple of congenial companions go hell for leather up and down the Junction with a brand new "*New Hope*" (but with a Big Engine Bolinder of course) and an equally youthful "*Fitton*".

After a few days I received the docking bill and now was my chance to recover the money Barlow's had fiddled me out of on the Leighton job, about £3 15s. I deducted this when I paid the bill and sent a covering letter explaining why. There followed an exchange of correspondence, each official letter from Barlows being accompanied by a personal one from David. It was all quite hilarious and eventually they backed down. This in no way affected my personal relationship with David and his delightful family, which was one of personal friendship coupled with a healthy prudence in matters of business. Not for nothing did irreverent boatmen refer to him as the One Armed Bandit. Anyway, he probably recovered the money on my refuelling bills.

Now back to work. Another load for Palmer's, which I had to unload by myself as Paddy was not to be found, followed by another Newdigate to Slough, notable for being done in three and a half days so I must have had most of the locks ready. Once emptied, I went straight down to Brentford and loaded tomato puree for Birmingham the following day. It was a British Waterways job arranged for me by Stan Argent, Willow Wren's manager at Brentford. First of all I had to call in at Bulls Bridge for the loan of a set of top cloths, all black and shiny, provoking comments from boatmen, "So that's where our best top cloths go!" The cargo was loaded at the Thames Steam Tug & Lighterage Company wharf in Brentford Creek below the Gauging lock. This was a 1930s style building with cranes on towers at each end of the warehouse. Jack Lane was there and I helped him stow his boats and then he helped me with mine. Rather than put the planks up on the stands my personal preference was to lay the middle plank on top of the cases, which are two tiers higher than the gunwhale and have the other planks sloping down from the mast and up to the cabin. I managed to get 23 tons 6 cwt on. *"New Hope"* had a long hold and puree is comparatively heavy as canned goods go.

This traffic arrived in London Docks every autumn in large quantities, requiring lots of boats and causing massive delays in unloading. I had been involved in it once before when working as a mate for George Smith. It was not surprising that I had a bad road all the way and took five days to get to Sampson Road in Birmingham . Such was the quantity of puree it had to be unloaded both there and at Warwick Wharf. It was four days before I got emptied but demurrage was paid for this. About this time British Waterways were sending spelter from London to Manchester. I believe one pair went via Fradley with forty tons but the others loaded fifty to fifty five tons and went via Birmingham, lightening into North Western Division boats at Sampson Road. I was there when young Jacky Lowe, son of 'Barnton Tommy' and by now a captain, arrived with his single motor to lighten the London boats and I helped a pair of the latter up to Farmer's Bridge to pass the time while waiting.

Morton had regained the Morrell's brewery (Oxford) traffic for the cut and I was pleased to get an order for this for my next trip. I bumped into George Element at Salford Bridge where, because it was Saturday, I stopped for the night. He asked me if I was interested in what we called the "top road" work which consisted of trips from Cannock to various factories in Upper Birmingham and from Holly Bank to Heaton & Dugards, a copper works in the Hospital Pound. I thought this would suit me very well and agreed to start when I came back from Oxford.

The trip from Griff to Oxford was as expected. The usual struggle with recalcitrant drawbridges, flushing out of Salmon's Lock, struggling down the Banbury Pound, "One foot of water and four feet of mud" and the long two day drag from Banbury to Oxford. On arrival I found that I had to unload myself. It was shovel and barrow using a plank to make a high pile so I asked the wharfinger to organise two blokes from the Labour Exchange and gave myself a rest, making the most of what was to be my last voyage to that city.

Below Hillmorton, on the way back, I met a pair of boats who told me that the Skinners were up the Rugby Arm. I reversed up the arm and helped them unload, towing them back to Suttons. This was to be the last load of coal Rose and Joe were to do; their long carrying career was now ended.

So that was the end of my work for Willow Wren. It was October and I didn't fancy the long trek singlehanded down to London in the winter months. It was hard and often awkward work, though perhaps I should have taken the advice of Freddie Morton who had been down there singlehanded during the war. He reckoned to tie up until a pair of boats came the other way and made some locks ready for him. Although there was some traffic offering on the Oxford I knew there would be no ice breaking if we had a bad freeze up. The B.C.N., and some quite substantial earnings, beckoned.

Entering Rickmansworth lock
with 23 tons of tomato puree
from Brentford to Birmingham.
(Mr. L.V. Reason)

Age 16 on *Columba*

Brasses and plates. *New Hope*'s cabin.

New Hope at Banbury with coal for Oxford.

Bar lock, Birmingham as I remember it.

New Hope at Hartshill.

Sherbourne Street wharf, Birmingham. The small jetty, middle left, was where coal for Hudson, Edmunds was unloaded.

Braunston puddle.

Unloading gantry at the GEC works, Witton.

Boatman's party at Bedworth.

Bottom of Napton locks.

Ling in Tardebigge locks bound for Worcester

Braunston Dock as it used to be. The station and signals can be seen in the background.

The boats are gone but the atmosphere is still there. Curdworth locks.

In Napton locks.

New Hope in Napton summit pound.

Rose and Joe Skinner with me in background

Empty boat in Fenny Tunnel straight

New Hope near Kirtlington

Sherbourne Street wharf. The boat is John Walley's *Blake.*

New Hope approaching Napton bottom lock.

New Hope at Fradley.

Only ten more to go! Going down Tardebigge locks in the rain.

Regent Swallow at Monk Meadow oil terminal, Gloucester. *(Port of Bristol Authority/Paul Barnett)*

Regent Robin. She could trade as far as Swansea in the summer months and was the first barge to which I was appointedf Mate/Driver. *(Port of Bristol Authority/Paul Barnett)*

Regent Swift in King Edward Lock, Avonmouth. The cylindrical object behind the tug *Resolute* is a dracone, conveying oil on an experimental trip to Gloucester. *(Port of Bristol Authority/Paul Barnett)*

Barges behind *SS Bristol City* in Avonmouth Docks, including two *Sabrina's* and two British Waterways motor barges. The *Sabrina* in the foreground has two portable rolling jacks (for moving the hold beams) laying on top of her hatch cloths. *(Port of Bristol Authority/Paul Barnett)*

A tow of barges leaving Avonmouth with *Sabrina 5* first behind the tug. Behind her is a barge loaded with logs for Lydney. *(Port of Bristol Authority/Paul Barnett)*

CHAPTER FIVE

Winter on the Top Road and a Summer's Pleasure Trips

I arrived at Salford Bridge on the 6th November, pleased to be back among all my old friends, and primed for action. Bright and early the next morning I started off up the New 'Uns on my way to Walsall Wood to load for the G.E.C. What a difference from the dreadful struggle up the Old Cut from Pooley. I loaded 23 tons instead of the 17 tons that I used to take from Pooley, went round the corner and tied up at the Travellers Rest, where I had the usual convivial evening, being down at the G.E.C. in time to unload the next day. Next I had orders for Cannock to load for Davenports brewery. I had a good day, going from the top of Mosses to the colliery, loading with 21 tons 10 cwt and tying up at the Bottom of Tipton Factory locks.

Why I went this way instead of by the more direct route via the Tame Valley I can't recall. Perhaps I was offered a boat to tow from Cannock or Pratts Bridge as sometimes happened. It's only three hours from the Factory to Davenports which was on the Worcester cut just through the first bridge from the Bar Lock. The site is now a block of yuppy flats. It was typical of many small works on the BCN, the coal being shovelled directly into the boiler room. It was this design of building, where the boiler room was inaccessible to lorries that kept so much traffic on the cut long after it might otherwise have been lost to road transport. In accordance with our arrangement, George sent me two men to help unload, and we managed this in a couple of hours so that I had a nice early night at the Bar Lock, with plenty of time to clean up, go shopping and make things ready for the next trip. Boatmen going to Davenport's received a beer allowance which was especially welcome in hot weather.

An early departure from the Bar lock took me to Holly Bank colliery basin at Short Heath, five miles beyond Wolverhampton which served Hilton Main Colliery. It was the first time I had loaded here and also the first time I had loaded out of boxes. The coal was brought down to the basin by the usual diminutive, shiny Coal Board steam loco. Each wagon held three boxes of coal, each box containing about two and a half tons. They were lifted by a crane, the bottom catch knocked out and the coal dropped in the boat. Nine boxes gave you about 22 tons. The coal was medium large lumps known as cobbles. I was soon to find that, when burnt on the cabin fire, Holly Bank coal produced copious quantities of soot.

Once again I tied at the bottom of the Factory, getting to Heaton & Dugard's, which was a copper works on the outside of the cut about half way down the Hospital Pound, and half emptying the following day. The coal had to be split between two unloading places, one of which required barrowing. There used to be an elevator at Heaton's but it had been allowed to fall into disrepair. The lack of simple machinery to assist in the tedious job of unloading coal was the norm at small works and wharves and never ceased to annoy me. I didn't mind shovelling if I had some help, it was good exercise and you had some company, but to empty a boat by yourself was a long and very tedious job.

We finished off the next day and went to pick up a boatload of ashes at Oozell Street which I towed to Oldbury. It was a Friday. The only colliery that loaded boats on Saturday was Brownhills so I went there and did a quick trip to Tyseley. I loaded and went to Salford Bridge, had a day off on Sunday (a day not usually worked by Joey boatmen although I sometimes did) and unloaded on Monday. Another shovel and barrow place, this time across the towpath, but here you did not have to unload yourself so, for a change, you could relax and watch someone else working.

Tuesday was a good day, Tyseley to Cannock, load and back to the top of Mosses. I had 23 tons on again for Davenports and all was going well until I got fast on the Tame Valley cut at Wednesbury at a point where a factory pumped sludge into the canal. British Waterways had inspectors who went round to all these factories, one of their jobs being to collect payment for taking water from the cut and discharging it back again. They knew perfectly well the amount of sediment that was being pumped back in but were apparently more interested in the water payments from these works, who did not use the cut for freight, than in the boat traffic. I was stuck there for an hour until a horse boat came along and pulled me through.

It was too late in the day for anyone to come down and help me unload so I started on it myself, finishing it off on the Thursday and going empty to Wolverhampton for an evening with my old mates on the Northern boats. Not that there were many there, traffic was quiet and they now waited for orders at Anderton rather than Wolverhampton. On Friday I loaded at Holly Bank for Heaton's and, as it was the weekend, spent it tied up at the Bar Lock, handy for shops, public baths and all the other attractions of Birmingham, such as they were in those days. The fortnight's work had earned me £43, fantastic money by canal standards for the amount of hours I had done. A round trip to Davenport's took about thirteen hours actual boating and one to Holly Bank twelve hours.

On the Monday I went down to Heaton & Dugard's where three of us soon got the boat emptied and I was down at Salford Bridge nice and early. To return to the collieries via Salford Bridge was the normal procedure after emptying in the Hospital Pound.

All went well for the next three months and the routine was varied by a trip to Hudson, Edmunds, a small copper works up the Oozell Street loop opposite Sherborne Street Wharf. Here there was a small landing stage on the towpath side and the coal, which was steam coal from Cannock, was barrowed into the works. There were no Waterways boats at Sherborne Street, how different from when I had first become acquainted with it in 1950 only seven years previously.

Another place I visited was British Industrial Plastics at Oldbury. I can't remember how I came to go there because the job was usually the preserve of Element's Oldbury tug. I had to go up the six Oldbury locks, known as the 'Crow'. These were surely the shortest locks on the B.C.N., requiring the removal of both of the tipcats in order to get the boat into each chamber. At the top was a very sharp turn, about 130 degrees, into the short Spon Lane Branch, always called the Feeder. Normally you would reverse up this arm for the short distance to the B.I.P. but, knowing *"New Hope's"* propensity to pick up rubbish in the blades when going astern loaded, I decided to wind, which meant shafting the fore end round as there was no room to manoeuvre. They already had a boat there so I didn't get unloaded until the next day giving me ample opportunity to explore this interesting, if unlovely part of Birmingham.

As usual at works like this, which employed hordes of women, I was bombarded with ribald suggestions at every shift change and meal break. Some of these girls had never seen a cabin boat at close quarters and wanted to have a look in the cabin. I was happy to oblige and had no difficulty in arranging a date for that evening. In those days working class people didn't have phones so you couldn't, as you would do nowadays, collect any phone numbers.

The unloading arrangements here were excellent. There was a vertical screw auger to lift the coal out of the hold. It was connected to a horizontal auger with controllable openings above the piles of coal in front of each boiler. The boat was emptied in short order, with the boat emptiers boasting about the efficiency of their apparatus.

I was enjoying this job; it gave me plenty of variety, taking me over nearly all the then navigable parts of the B.C.N. with whose never ending fascination I had an ongoing love affair. How I loved the damp, misty mornings when flames came out of the chimney when you lit the fire and there was a shot of rum in the first mug of tea; and the frosty evenings, boating along in the dark with a huge fire under your feet, the gramophone on the cabin top and a piece of prime steak in the oven.

As it happened, I wasn't able to delight in what we called the Top Road very much longer as changes were afoot.

Around this time George Element was able to make a start on mechanising the Salford Bridge traffic. This came about because Billy Randle, an Oldbury boatman with a reputation for hard work, expressed an interest in the *"Mayflower"*, an ex-Grand Union Ricky motor like *"New Hope"*. *"Mayflower"* had been employed on the Stourport Light job and when that finished in 1949 was used for a while on Salford Bridge traffic under the captaincy of Alfie Ray. She used to start the week with a trip to the Tame & Ray District Drainage Board wharf at Minworth where she loaded sand for Camp Hill. After this had been discharged with a shovel and barrow she spent the rest of the week on coal from Pooley. She had not lasted long on the Bottom Road (I wonder why!) and had been laid up at Oldbury for years.

Billy, who worked with his wife, immediately set to work on the G.E.C. job, doing five trips a week.

"Mayflower" had the same National engine in her as when she was bought from the Grand Union and I wasn't surprised when, one day when I was tied up at Salford Bridge, George appeared and asked me if I knew anything about Nationals. I forebore from telling him that I didn't *want* to know anything about them and, although my knowledge of those engines was confined to being aware of the nasty tricks they could play, I agreed to go and have a look. *"Mayflower"* was tied up at the G.E.C. Following a hunch I suggested to Billy that he took the cylinder head off. My suspicions were correct. The small object, rather like the top of a Brasso tin, on top of one of the pistons had worked loose, hit the head and smashed the top of the piston. A new piston was obtained and put in and off went Billy hell for leather.

A week later *"Mayflower"* broke down again and, when I was on my way to the collieries, I was told to stop at Walsall Wood and tow her to Oldbury for which I was paid £3. This was on the 22nd December, a Sunday, so it was a bit of extra pay. Having left Billy at Oldbury and returned empty to Wolverhampton, I put a load in for Heaton's, going down as far as Salford Bridge where I remained for Christmas. You had to be careful about where you left a load of coal unattended and she was safe enough at Salford Bridge while I went home for the holiday.

I resumed the normal routine after Christmas with the exception that I had a load of ashes from Davenports which was to be emptied on the towpath at Coseley. Ashes were in regular demand for towpath maintenance and the carriers got paid twice, once for removing them and again for placing them conveniently to make up the towpath. I had assistance to unload and load at the brewery and my temporary mate came with me to Coseley which was conveniently on the way to his home at Wolverhampton. As we unloaded the coal, loaded and unloaded the ashes in one day this was highly profitable, £9 being paid to me for the ash job.

Removing these ashes became a regular task for me after this.

The next trip was from Cannock to Baxters' Nile Street nut and bolt works, on the main line where it cut off the Oozell Street loop. This was better paid than Davenports although the coal had to be barrowed out. I liked Baxter's even when, as later happened, I had to unload there by myself because it was out on the main line and you could see all the traffic going by. It was rare to see another boat while at Davenport's.

Came the end of January and it was becoming difficult to find assistance for emptying. I found myself without any help on the next trip to Heaton & Dugard's. It was a horrible place to empty single handed. As it happened I had enough to do with Davenports and Baxters' and Billy Randle wanted the Heaton's job so that was the last time I went there. A pity, it was an easy and profitable trip provided you had some help to unload.

The routine was broken by being sent empty from Baxters' to Walsall Wood where there was a boat which required towing in to the G.E.C. Albert was waiting for me at the Wood and it made a nice change to have another boatman to help me move the recalcitrant wagons and help me load. When we got down to the G.E.C. a spell of ice set in and I did some work loading boats at Saltley Sidings and a short trip to the Premier Electric at the top of Saltley locks.

Back on the top road, I was now unloading twice a week by myself, except for one occasion when Brian Cusack came with me for a trip. It must have been the Easter school holidays. He frightened the life out of me on this occasion. We had partially unloaded at Davenport's and when I woke up the next morning he was nowhere to be seen. Of course I was scared that he might have fallen in the cut but eventually he reappeared having got up early and gone for a "wander round".

On another occasion at the same place I was shovelling away when I heard the unmistakeable sound of a nine horse Bolinder approaching. The "Chiltern", captained by my old friend Jim, appeared and he kindly stopped and helped me finish the coal and load the ashes. Jim was on his way to Tyseley with milk powder from Worcester so, in return, I helped him down the Thirteen and Deritend locks. I intended to go with him to the top of Camp Hill but they were locked up for the night when we got to the bottom. Jim kindly allowed me to steer and strap so I was able to add another boat to the list of those I had handled. I saw Jim again a few weeks later when we were able to tie up together at the Bar Lock. It was the last time I would see him for many years.

Things were changing. George decided to give Billy Randle the Davenport's work leaving me with Baxters' and trips to either the G.E.C. or Tyseley. I didn't mind this as I had become pally with a lad at Walsall Wood who introduced me to the delights of the Sunday afternoon session at the Avion Cinema at Aldridge, to which place there was a convenient bus. The Avion was one of those cinemas (or picture houses as we used to call them) where boy met girl. The girls would go with their mates but sit alone.

You would ask them if they were by themselves, if the girl liked the look of you she would say "Yes". Then you would ask if you could sit by her and, if she agreed, it was the expected thing that kissing and cuddling would take place. The second time I went I met a nice young lady from Norton Canes and I joined Marie every weekend after that.

My friend Baz was actually still at school but he was built like the side of a house like so many teenagers in an age of unlimited food and relatively high incomes. If his tales were to be believed he enjoyed frequent and varied sexual experiences, which, in the 1950's, were not all that easily come by. In the holidays he would borrow a horse and cart, buy a load of coal with his uncle's licence, and go round the streets selling it. Baz was just one of the colourful characters at the Wood, all of whom I knew well.

People may think I am mad but I would far sooner spend an evening in a pub like the Traveller than in any of the tarted up and expensive places that most canal side pubs have become. If you tied up here with a load of nuts or big coal shadowy figures would appear on the towpath after dark and ask to fill their washtubs. Why, I wondered, were ladies always sent to do this job?

I knew that work would dry up around Birmingham by the end of April so I had already made arrangements for the summer. Bert Dunkley was going to organise a season of pleasure boat trips and Joe Skinner and I had agreed to do them. This was better, I thought, than struggling down the Junction singlehanded which appeared to be the only other work around.

Meanwhile I carried on while work was available and, one day, I was sent to the Midland Counties Dairy in the Hospital Pound to load rubbish. Cakey came with me and we shovelled the rubbish over from a boat that was kept moored there permanently. It was mostly packing materials and empty containers, a "load of wind" as we called these light but bulky cargoes.

After emptying at Moxley tip I went up Walsall locks. Standing on the lockside at the top lock was the portly figure of Handel

James. Handel was in charge of toll and rent collection on the B.C.N. but that day, he had other things on his mind.

"We're desperate for a load of coal to the Porcelain. Will you do one?"

Here was a bolt from the blue. I didn't know Handel had become involved with the Porcelain traffic. He was shortly to add the task of Fleet Superintendent of the Midland Fleet to his duties. I am not sure exactly when this fleet was set up but, at the time, the Worcester traffic had to rely mainly on Northern boats and that Division would only provide them when they had no other work. Having been 'manoeuvred', to use a polite expression, out of this job in 1956 I was rather surprised to be asked to help them out. I agreed to go subject to immediate unloading. I had a date with Marie that Sunday and wanted to be back in Birmingham to catch the bus to Aldridge.

The Porcelain coal now came from Cannock instead of Brownhills. I made short work of getting to Worcester, meeting Jumbo Harris in the '30' with a load of milk powder. He now had a proper butty, the South Western division having put a cabin on one of their station boats. I was surprised, when I arrived there to find an unfamiliar and apparently deserted boat lying there loaded. She was the "*Arcturus*" and her owners had been doing some part time boating, going down loaded one weekend, lying at Worcester all week, and going up empty the next weekend. I was furious that this work, which I greatly coveted, had been given to amateur boatmen instead of being offered to somebody like me who had to make a living. Although, thinking with the benefit of hindsight, I should have kept in touch with events, found out that Mr Oxley was retiring and applied to his replacement for reinstatement on the contract. The trouble was that news circulated very inefficiently among the waterway community in the days before magazines like "*Waterways World*" kept everyone in touch with events. In any case, one was so busy boating that it was hard to distinguish the wood from the trees.

"Arcturus" was pulled out of the length and in went *"New Hope"* to be swiftly unloaded and soon racing hell for leather back to Birmingham. I got to the Bar Lock on Sunday morning just in time to wash and change, catch the bus to Aldridge and sink into the fleshly delights of the Avion Cinema.

I had a message at Birmingham from David Campbell asking me to go to Middleport. The Anderton Company's dockyard had just closed and Barlows had bought a lot of the equipment and needed it transported to Braunston. It was a pity I hadn't known this earlier as I could have gone back up the Stour cut. As it was I had made the long climb up to Birmingham and now had to go down Wolverhampton locks, making the Cross Keys at Filance that night and Stoke the next.

Philip Shirley was on the dock, overseeing the sad procedure of closing down the dockyard. His company, the Mersey, Weaver & Ship Canal Carrying Co., had just been sold to British Waterways, although he was to retain some of the warehouses in his own name. We chatted and he told me that the trade in pottery materials, brought by sea to the Mersey and then by canal to the Potteries, had been ruined by road haulage direct from Cornwall.

This was to be my last carrying trip over the North Stafford. As I wended my way down the Trent Valley with the hold full of a variety of boatbuilding equipment, which Mr Shirley had carefully instructed me to declare as "scrap" for toll purposes, I cast my mind back to the first time I had seen this cut, in February 1950. Then John Knill and I had been full of optimism for the future of canal carrying but now all was gloom. I stopped at Rugeley for the night, catching the bus to Aldridge that Sunday afternoon for my last ever date with Marie.

When I reached Glascote, the foreman of S.E. Barlow's dock asked me if he could have a few bits and pieces out of the cargo. Knowing they had not been itemised I agreed and in return he gave me a painted cabin stool which I still have.

After unloading at Braunston, I oiled up, and went back to Sutton's. During that summer the Skinners and I did two or three trips a week carrying passengers in our scrubbed out holds. Some were school trips and others were for various organisations, all ably organised by the late Bert Dunkley. My favourite was the Young Farmers Club who boasted several delightful lasses among their company. We didn't earn a great deal of money, but it was enough to live on and there was hardly any wear and tear on the boats. We would usually go to Stretton or Newbold, occasionally to Griff. During the summer holidays, Bert organised a camping trip with young people sleeping under the canvas cloths, separated by the Dunkley Patent Sex Separator which consisted of a sheet of hessian. Ray's boats were tied up for the holiday. We invited him to come with us but he wouldn't. However, his mate Kath, with whom I was, at the time greatly smitten, decided to come. We spent a fortnight going to Penkridge and back. It was a very enjoyable trip, starting from Coventry Basin, the first time I had ever been there. We made a prolonged stop at Milford where there was a funfair. Returning from this, we did another long trip to Banbury and back.

CHAPTER SIX

Sunshine

Came September with an autumnal nip in the air and I decided to see what George Element had to offer for the winter. The Gas Board were in the process of laying a pipeline under the towpath to serve their Windsor Street works at Aston. This meant large quantities of spoil had to be boated away from the site. This was thrown out into the cut along a portion of the 'Edgeford Arm that was suffering badly from subsidence. George loved this sort of job. He got paid for removing the spoil and again for supplying it to the British Waterways engineering department.

I did my first trip that winter on September 16th with one of Element's boats with spoil for Moxley. The next trip, with "New Hope", was sand from Oozell Street to Winson Green towing an open boat. After that there were several trips with spoil to Churchbridge, back loading with slack from Walsall Wood to the G.E.C. Sometimes I had to spend the night at Churchbridge, on this part of the canal you were high up and got the most marvellous, lurid sunsets, the sort that only the smoky air of the Black Country could produce. I loved to stand in the doorholes, watching the sunset in the peace and quiet of the evening after work had finished, smoking a contemplative cigarette while the smell of supper cooking rose from the cabin.

The spoil job lasted into October. Then it was coal to the G.E.C. with the occasional empty boat, hired for the spoil contract from Jimmy Yates, to tow back to Norton Canes. Loading at Walsall Wood was as tiresome as ever and made worse by the fact that the basin there was now badly silted thus reducing payloads. For some reason I can no longer remember, I made one round trip with a horseboat, out with rubbish to Moxley and back with coal to the

G.E.C., followed by a trip to the Wood and back towing a joey boat.

On the 20th October there was good news. The coal allocation for the G.E.C. had been moved from Walsall Wood Colliery to Holly Bank. Hooray! No more struggling to move railway trucks about with a pinch-bar and then shovelling the coal into the boat. Holly Bank was a holiday compared to the Wood. The rate dropped of course, but only from 7s to 6s 6d and it was possible to do four trips a week if I really wanted to. By unloading the first boat at the G.E.C., having winded at Salford Junction beforehand, it was often possible to load at Holly Bank that same afternoon. I rarely did more than three, which brought me in over £20 per week. The rate increased to 6s 9d per ton early in 1959.

I enjoyed this run but it had its problems. Going through Friar Park there was a high bridge, providing an excellent opportunity for the local kids to throw missiles at the boatmen, safe in the knowledge that we couldn't get at them. On one occasion I was aground under this bridge while the kids were trying to drop sheets of corrugated iron onto the boat. Fortunately none of them hit the target. There was no problem during school hours but school holidays were at nightmare. I soon learned to arrange my loaded journeys so as to go through here either very early in the morning or late at night, tying up at Ocker Hill Power Station for a few hours if necessary.

One week in the school holidays I had the pleasure of the company of Baz Blakemore, from Walsall Wood so I had a bit of a holiday myself not having to get the locks ready.

It was at Holly Bank that I had what might have been a serious accident. I had arrived there after dark and tied up alongside an empty boat. Later on in the evening I went outside to chop some firewood on the wharf. A thick fog had descended and, having forgotten that I had tied up alongside another boat, I took its gunwhale to be the wooden edge of the wharf. Chopper in one hand and a bike torch in the other, I confidently stepped, as I supposed, ashore only to fall the four feet into the other boat's hold. I was pretty shaken up but fortunately escaped with a few cuts and bruises.

If I had to oil up I would detour via Brownhills and take on fuel from Yate's tank. I often tied up at the top of Mosses on these occasions. Bobby had moved his houseboat and was now moored there, and he was always entertaining company. One day I discovered he had a motor boat tied alongside. She was the *"Sunshine"*. Bobby told me that Potter & Sons had ceased carrying and he had gone to Runcorn and bought her. I was quite taken with this boat, not least by the fact that she had a Bolinder engine, so I decided to buy her. It wasn't a good idea, it would have been more sensible to spend the money on *"New Hope"*, but I couldn't resist having something different to play with.

I didn't intend to sell *"New Hope"* at that time and kept both boats for a while. I loaded *"Sunshine"* for the first time on December 29th 1958. She had a longer cabin than my other boat but it had a little less headroom. The door-holes were about 6 inches lower than those on *"New Hope"* and I felt uncomfortably exposed when steering. She was a smaller boat. The most I ever got on her was 22 tons 15 cwt. She was undoubtedly the worst steering boat I ever had, having to keep going forward and astern to get round the junction of the Walsall canal and the Tame Valley Canal; and the 20hp Bolinder, which had a gear box rather than being a direct reversing engine, was far too powerful for a single motor on a shallow cut, but she was a pretty boat with shapely lines and I loved her. The only advantage was that she was so heavy in the stern that she could tow two loaded boats without being loaded herself. This proved advantageous as I could tow rubbish boats to Moxley, returning with a coal boat from Holly Bank. Sometimes I would tow a couple of loaded boats round from Saltley sidings to the G.E.C.

It was while towing a boat from Holly Bank that I experienced having a bottom knocked up. This was not uncommon on what were, by now, appallingly badly maintained cuts. I knew of a pair of boats that had hit a sunken safe in Barnton tunnel, knocking up some bottoms in both boats and of another that had hit an obstruction in Tipton Old 'Uns. My mate, Jim, driving into a lock near the top of 'Hampton had suffered the same fate. Having this happen was dreaded by everyone because the boat, engine hole and cabin would fill with water.

It was a bitterly cold April day and we were creeping along the New Cut which was so shallow you couldn't go very fast. Charlie Foster had come aboard to steer "Sunshine" while I cooked my breakfast. His son, Horace, was on the joey boat. We were just past the Walsall Road Bridge at Stone Cross when the boat came to a stop. I stepped ashore and walked up to the fore-end. Looking into the hold I was alarmed to find it full of water up to the lining piece. The boat couldn't sink altogether as she had dropped onto the bottom of the cut.

Fortune was with me that day. "Sunshine's" back end stank was watertight up to gunwhale height so no water could get into the engine-hole or the cabin.

Finding the nearest public call box, I phoned British Waterways and then George Element. Sunken boats were routine on the B.C.N. and rescue was swiftly organised. It was a very cold day and a bitter east wind howled unimpeded over the exposed embankment. Cakey Bill was the first to arrive on the scene, with orders to buy us all a drink. George sent an empty boat up from Salford Bridge and, once it arrived, we quickly transhipped "Sunshine's" cargo of slack This revealed no less than five bottoms knocked up. The damage was covered with a thick layer of clay. By the time we had done this it was late and, having decided to have the repairs done at Jimmy Yates' dock, I was advised to spend the night in the bottom pound of the Ganzy. We drained the pound and let the boat lie on the bottom so that she would be in no danger of sinking during the night.

Jimmy Yates put the boat on the dry dock immediately and soon had five new bottoms put in. This cost over £70 of which

British Waterways, although they were at fault, would agree to pay no more than half. I did a couple of trips with *"New Hope"* while *"Sunshine"* was on the dock. British Waterways dragged the place where I had hit the obstacle and recovered a 'tank trap' from the cut. These were triangular lumps of concrete designed to disable tanks had there been an invasion during World War Two. They were very heavy and it was difficult to imagine how one could have been manoeuvred into the water.

On cold, frosty nights I would experiment with different varieties of coal so as to get the range as hot as possible while going along the Tame Valley. Playing about like this one evening I forgot that I had a piece of steak in the oven and found it charred to a crisp when I tied up at the top of Perry Bar. I would also put the gramophone on the cabin top and play records while going along to relieve the monotony of steering along miles of straight, shallow canal, the engine barely ticking over to avoid hitting the bottom.

At the end of April the winter coal allocations finished. I had already arranged to do some more day trips for Bert Dunkley during the summer of 1959 so I set off down the Fazeley cut with Bobby's houseboat in tow. He had been offered a free mooring in Wyken basin, which was then being dredged, in return for acting as watchman. In the meantime he moored at the end of the Griff arm.

Once more I was working with the Skinner's who, as always, were congenial company. We would make our usual expeditions on Joe's brakeless bikes, roam Courtauld's tip looking for anything useful and I would be roped in to turn the mangle on washday, done in the traditional manner with a fire, washtub and dolly peg on the towpath. We paid a visit to Foleshill Gasworks and came back with enough drums of tar to black our boats round.

By this, his second year of retirement, Joe had rescued a huge pile of fire-wood from the cut, sawn it up and kept it under a canvas cover on the towpath.

I had scraped up an acquaintance with a young lady from Walsgrave, a girl whose ultimate fantasy was to drive a double decker bus at 60 mph down the newly opened M1 Motorway. We went out for a few months but, apart from not sharing her taste in speedway racing, she would never agree to going into a pub for a drink. Being a Sunday School teacher seemed to have something to do with this though it didn't seem to inhibit her in other ways. Rose and Joe came to the rescue and when I arrived home I would always find a bottle of Atkinson's Old just inside the cabin door. She also had the disconcerting habit of engaging in an amorous clinch just before my last bus home was due. Time after time I missed the bus and had to walk back to the Stop, a journey which included the wooded lane of Wyken Croft which had a bad reputation after dark though it just seemed a pleasant walk to me.

The pleasure boat trips were erratic and if there were a few days without one I would go for a boat trip with one of my mates. On one occasion I went with Charlie to Nash Mills. While we were waiting to unload I got into conversation with a girl and we went for a walk down the towpath. Returning just in time for a drink at the pub I was seized upon by Charlie and his mates.

"Let's have a look at your hands."

"Why?"

"We want to see if there's any nylon under your fingernails."

This girl persuaded me to take a small dog off her hands. I took it back to Sutton's where it was promptly adopted by Rose and Joe who named it Scruffy.

It was during this summer that we had a foretaste of things to come in the canal world. It had always been the custom to allow retired boatmen to live in a boat anywhere on the cut that suited them and there were several such boats at Sutton's beside Joe's and mine. We had a visit from an intrepid young man from the South Eastern Divisional traffic office at Birmingham who announced that, as we had not been working recently, we would have to pay a mooring fee.

This news did not meet with a warm reception. There were angry protests and one aged boatman drew himself up to his full height, fixed the youth with a piercing blue eye and pronounced the ultimate anathema.

"I was working on this yere cut when your arsehole warn't no bigger'n a shirt button!"

The young man slunk away defeated. Joe and I paid a visit to Sampson Road to see Mr Gregory, the Divisional Traffic Officer and our arguments won the day. For the time being there were to be no mooring fees.

It was during this summer that I met the girl who was to become my future wife. Rose and Joe had often expressed the view that it was time I met "Mrs Right". One day Joe told me there was a girl he wanted me to meet. We set off walking along the towpath until we came to a strange looking horse boat, converted into a floating Youth Hostel. This was the *"Margaret"*, owned by Pat Saunders and working between Oxford, Llangollen and Manchester.

In answer to Joe's hail a vision in tight, white shorts appeared and invited us aboard for lunch. We struck up an immediate rapport and, as far as the exigencies of being always on the move allowed, started to go out together. On one occasion a group of us decided to visit Jane Nixon who now lived in a caravan at Longford. We were taken there in an open motor boat, with a piece of canvas pulled over us as it was raining heavily.

"Margaret" usually moored at Tushes Bridge and I was able to show Jeanne the "short cut" through the fields behind the back of the Power Station. This establishment was so iconic of our courting days that we heard of its demolition with some sadness.

CHAPTER SEVEN

Pastures New

As summer drew to an end I started to think about the winter's trading. I was on the lookout for a better boat than "*Sunshine*" and the towpath grapevine rumoured that British Waterways Midland Fleet wanted to sell the "*Ling*". A former northern Josher, she had been bought by the Midland fleet who had replaced her pup Bolinder by a 'big engine' to allow her to pull a butty. The engine was a good one and had been taken out of the "*Gorse*", one of the last Joshers to be built.

I went over to their headquarters at Worcester Wharf, Birmingham and saw Handel James, who had added the job of Fleet Superintendent to his other work. He explained that he didn't want to sell "*Ling*" but was looking for a Captain for her and would I like the job? Subconsciously I must have been ready to give up working for myself as I immediately expressed an interest.

At that moment, who should come into the office after a job but my erstwhile mate on the "*Fitton*". I hadn't seen him since he disappeared at Hayes Cocoa with the shopping money, leaving his wife behind. Handel got rid of him quickly and made a few caustic remarks about his character. Evidently he was well known among canal employers.

It was lunchtime so Handel suggested we adjourn to the Crown in Broad Street. Over a pint he explained the rates of pay which I thought were generous by boating standards. The coal for the Worcester Porcelain works was now being drawn from Cannock & Rugeley Colliery at Hednesford Basin and the rate was 6s 1d per ton with empty boat money of 30s. Return loads to Sherborne Street were 5s per ton and to Tyseley 5s 6d. So-called "District money" for boats unloading in Birmingham and going empty to the collieries was 15s. Unloading at Worcester was 3s per ton. Stowing and discharging of general cargo was paid at 3s 3d per hour. The fall back, below which your wages could not drop, was £3.15s per week.

I agreed to take the job and matters were finalised by a few words with George Cox, the South Western Division District Traffic Officer. British Waterways had an abundance of "Officers" of one description or another and there sometimes seemed to be more Chiefs than Indians. But George Cox was very well respected and had recently obtained quite a bit of new traffic for the cut which made him well liked by the boatmen.

On the train back to Coventry (a "*Jubilee*" hauled steam train, of course) I reflected on the day's events and felt I had made the right decision. I had made a good living out of being an owner boatman but, every time I got a job I could really enjoy, it seemed to be snatched away by events. I didn't really enjoy working on the short distance coal and rubbish jobs around Birmingham which were more suitable for boatmen who did not live aboard, nor did I like working the "Junction" with a single boat. The Worcester run had always been my favourite because the cut was easy to work single- handed and offered plenty of variety.

Back at Sutton's I kicked off "*Sunshine*" and headed towards Brum., making Salford Bridge that night and spending the evening among my old mates in the Muckman. I was at Bridge Street by around 9 am the next morning, laying "*Sunshine*" alongside the "*Ling*". As was customary, I scrubbed the "*Ling*'s" cabin out thoroughly before moving my stuff aboard, a good fire in the range soon dried the cabin out. Then I transferred all my "cabin things", hung up my curtains and plates and polished all the brasses. I checked the hold, all was in order except for the absence of top cloths. The cratch was already up and decorated with the usual scrubbed white piece of canvas hosepipe and cotton strings. The cabin chimney had been left with its brass rings and brass safety chain. Then it was time for the engine hole and there she lay... a magnificent 15hp single cylinder, direct-reversing, blowlampstarting Bolinder, all mine to play with. Bolinders, to me, had the same appeal as motor bikes to other young men. The noise, the vibration, the sheer rhythm of these wonderful machines was my idea of heaven. I lost no time in "putting the lamp on", finding it easy to start and reversing perfectly.

Handel had kindly allowed me to leave "*Sunshine*" under the warehouse canopy, the warehouses at Bridge Street being now used by lorry traffic only. I reported to his office to let him know I was ready. He said I could leave for Hednesford right away but first invited me over to the Crown. I mentioned the lack of top cloths and was told some were on order. Handel told me that Harry, "*Ling*'s" previous Captain had sold the top cloths and also the dynamo before leaving. He suspected that a deal had been done at a pub of some disrepute in Worcester known as the *Potters Arms*. It was suggested that I should visit the *Potters Arms* and see if I could find out anything about the theft. There was no way I was going to get involved in this but I was diplomatic and made the right noises before downing my pint and hastening to enjoy kicking off my new toy and heading for Hednesford.

I had never visited Hednesford, known to boatmen as 'Edgeford, before. The basin, adjacent to Cannock Wood basin, lay at the end of the 'Edgeford Arm, in other words the Cannock Extension Canal, sometimes known as the 'eavitup' from the practice of boatmen meeting other boats shouting 'eavitup' as a request for the oncoming boat to lift its line over the other rather than one of them having to carry out the official instructions to stop the horse and let the line drop in the water for the other boat to float over it.

It was dusk when I arrived. There was a solitary cabin boat amongst all the waiting joey boats and a head popped out of the cabin and urged me to tie alongside. This turned out to be Vern Nixon, one of the 14 offspring of 'Jumpabout Ernie' and Jane Nixon. We went up to the pub and Vern told me all about the job. Boats were loaded at Hednesford by the crane and box method in the same way I have described for Holly Bank. This meant that all the coal had to be loaded in the middle of the hold with the stands removed so the planks were laid on top of the cargo sloping up to the mast at one end and to the engine-hole roof at the other. Next day we loaded and went to Birmingham, thence to the bottom of Astwood (known as Ernie's Lock after its lock keeper Ernie Garrett). From there we went to Worcester and started to unload our two boats.

When I had been to the Porcelain before there had been unloaders so this was the first time I had to unload myself. As usual there was nowhere near enough room on the wharf and we had to climb the mountain of slack and shovel some coal back to make room. The boiler man was very good and would always shovel a path through to the canal side during the night rather than taking the nearest coal. This gave us a bit of room in the morning.

Vern and I were often in each other's company. We tried several pubs before settling on the Old Rectifying House on the Quay and another pub called the Shades. The Shades had a music room and it was popular with girls. The landlady kindly warned us about girls who drank at your expense all evening and then, on pretence of visiting the toilet, disappeared just before closing time.

I was lucky on that first trip being offered a load of sultanas for Sherborne Street. We overcame the temporary absence of top cloths by borrowing some lorry sheets! Sultanas were a seasonal traffic at this time of the year, being brought from Australia and put in barges at Avonmouth for Worcester. They had to be fumigated which was done by lifting up a barge hatch slightly and inserting a pipe through which gas was pumped. The rate was 5s per ton with 14s 2d for stowing the cargo at Worcester and about the same for helping unload at Birmingham. There was some delay at Sherborne Street as I received two days 'laying money'. You had to be delayed for three days before you were entitled to this payment but two of these were the weekend for which we were paid as it was a seven day a week job.

"*Ling*" proved to be a convenient boat, easily able to carry 22 tons on this route. She had the advantage of not being overlong which was useful as we went via West Bromwich Eight locks which were rather short. Although she didn't have a balanced rudder she was easy enough to steer, far better than my first Josher the "*Eagle*", which was a heavy old thing, and infinitely superior to the "*Sunshine*". "*Ling*" was originally built with a fore cabin but this had been removed which I thought spoiled her appearance.

The only problem I encountered with her was the small 50 gallon fuel tank, big engines normally having a 100 gallon tank. It meant that oiling up, which was now done at Broad Street, Wolverhampton, had to take place every trip and a half, she had not quite enough capacity to do two trips. I didn't mind the detour via Wolverhampton when I was empty but it lost a lot of time when loaded compared to the direct route via the Walsall Canal. I was dismayed to find that while Broad Street had oil and lube there was no soft soap or wipers available as there used to be when we oiled up at Albion Wharf. Eventually I got a bag of rags for engine cleaning and I had to buy the soft soap, which was used on cylinder head 'joints' (or gaskets) as well as hand cleaning and take the bill to the office.

On my next trip down to Worcester I encountered Johnny Anderson who had the "*Prince Charles*". He was just tying up above the Halfway Lock in the Tardebigge flight; this being the nearest point to Bromsgrove Station, explaining he was off to Sutton's to see his girlfriend. John didn't stay much longer with our fleet and his boat, together with the butty "*Jesmond*" was taken over by Joe and Polly Safe with their son Joey and Tommy Lowe for a mate. They lent me a very nice, solid brass short exhaust pipe and cutter. We also carried a long pipe for use when the engine was idling for a long period but I never used it. Also on the job were Teddy (Beck) Bickerton and family with "*Nautilus*" and "*Altair*".

On discharging my next load of coal at Worcester, and by now having a spanking new set of green top cloths, I had a load of tins of tomatoes for Tyseley. Here I became acquainted with the dilatory attitude of this depot had to its canal trade. Reporting to the office one would be greeted by a sigh of exasperation and an irritated "Why can't they send it by road?" The trouble was that by now each depot was a 'profit centre' and it was quicker and therefore cheaper to unload lorries. Added to this was the fact that Tyseley belonged to the South Eastern Division whereas our Worcester boats were in the South Western. It was the latter that bore the costs of delays. Such nonsense's were not confined to inter-Divisional matters. Our boats, coming under the Midland District were not allowed to refuel at the Severn District maintenance yard on the river at Worcester. On this occasion I spent three and a half days at Tyseley, being unloaded just in time to avoid the firm paying laying money.

All these cargoes of cased goods had to be stacked high to get a full load on so it was possible to dispense with the stands and support all the planks behind the mast on the cases. I never adopted the traditional practice of using all the top strings. It wasn't necessary, you spliced a top string to each cloth, brought it back to the next ring behind, then back through the next ring forward , over the plank, through the opposite ring, then through the opposite eye, then through the ring nearest opposite that and then the usual hitch on top of the plank. This stretched each sheet back and held down the front of the sheet behind over which the string passed. An additional string had to be used at the rear of the back-end cloth. I never found clothing up or un-sheeting singlehanded at all difficult despite the heavy and unwieldy cloths and I was surprised that the wartime women trainees have gone into print to tell us how much they used to dread this job.

Perhaps I should have tried to enjoy the enforced rest but at the age of 26 I was always eager to get going. Anyway, Tyseley was a particularly dull and unlovely suburb of Birmingham, far from the city centre.

From Tyseley the route to the colliery lay via Camp Hill locks, Salford Bridge and the Tame Valley and Walsall Canals. It would have been slightly shorter to go via Walsall Wood but the Walsall Canal route avoided having to dismantle the cratch for the extremely low railway bridge at the Wood. I was lucky, all the time I had *"Ling"* I never had to dismantle her cratch as one frequently had to do on other routes. I did have to lower one of the pounds in Tipton Factory locks a couple of times to get under a bridge, and once, during bridge repairs at Darlaston, I had to persuade all the workmen to get on the deck so I could get under. I usually managed to spend the night at Salford Bridge, giving all my old mates a chance to admire my smart boat and to have a few pints with them in the Muckman.

There was still an adequate depth of water throughout most of the Worcester cut although the Salt Pound, which extends for about a mile below Hammond's Lock was slow going. The worst section was the Lowesmoor pound, a mile of rubbish infested mud and water below Bilton locks. After a memorable occasion when Vern and myself had a particularly difficult struggle up here with two loads of tomato puree for Fazeley Street we adopted the practice, when we had uphill loads, of tying up for the night above the Blockhouse lock rather than in Diglis Basin. This gave all night for the pound to fill up after we had drawn four deep locks-full of water off it. It was amazing what difference an extra inch or two of water made. Coming down wasn't so much of a problem as downhill boats were carrying the water with them but you had to be careful so as to avoid a bladeful of rubbish.

We didn't get through the winter without ice and Joe Safe and I were given a sound telling off by a lady on a plywood pleasure boat moored at Hanbury Wharf who wanted to know why we couldn't wait for the icebreaker. Polly's colourful retort will not bear repeating. This was a new one on me but we were used to complaints from the fishermen who wanted to know why we had to work on Sundays.

On one trip I made some extra money towing a boat down to Hanbury Wharf, an old Shropshire Union boat without a rudder. I got Bernard to come with me and we made £4 apiece. On another occasion, a weekend, I took Bernard, his wife Mary and Albert Barlow for a trip. Leaving the Bar lock at midday Saturday we worked nonstop through the night to Worcester, pausing only for a pint at the Halfway House, arriving at Worcester early in the morning and being unloaded by 9 am on Sunday morning.

On another occasion, following a severe downpour, I left Birmingham, again at midday expecting to tie up at the Halfway. On the west side of Shortwood tunnel there is a storm drain which had thrown a bar of mud across the cut. There I had to stay until Tardebigge yard sent some assistance. This wasn't the only troublesome storm drain. There was one between King's Head and Blockhouse locks which eventually made so bad a scour that uphill loaded boats had to have a flush from the Blockhouse to get over it. This made getting away from Worcester a tiresome procedure. First of all Danny Merrill would have to be asked to help me up the two barge locks because there was no way a single handed boatman could get ashore to work them. There were no lock ladders in those days. Going down wasn't a problem because you could use a thumb string to open a bottom gate.

Having got into Kings Head lock, it was then necessary to walk up to Billy Russell's house at the Blockhouse and ask him to draw a flush, that is to say, raise the paddles and drop them again, thus creating a wave to get me over the bar. On the subject of the two barge locks, it was difficult to line the boat up to enter them from the river if there was any fresh and if there were barges moored abreast immediately below. On one occasion the current held me across the bows of a row of barges and I had to be pulled into the lock by one of the road vehicle tractor units. Going down I once sailed out when the water was so high that I didn't need to work the bottom lock.

The routine continued, coal to the Porcelain and some return loads back to Birmingham until December when Vern and I were told to load turf from a field between the bottom of Astwood and Hanbury Wharf. The turf from this field was sold to a landscaping firm for making lawns. I had to unload mine above Jill's (the bottom two locks of the Perry Bar flight) while Vern had to unload above Smethwick top lock. I had no idea how heavy this turf was so started to load at the back of the mast and worked backwards. I hadn't realised that *"Ling"* had dropped on the bottom while loading. When I pushed her off she dropped alarmingly and had very little dry side. I had her gauged at the top of Tardebigge and found she had 24 tons on. The most I had ever brought up previously was 22 tons.

However all went well until Cuckoo Bridge in Aston Locks where she firmly stuck until the arrival of a downhill boat gave her a lock-full of water that flushed her off. As I steered round the junction at Salford Bridge, George Element appeared outside his office, eyes a-goggle at what was, for that area and type of boat, an enormous overload. Getting through Salford Bridge stop place was another struggle after which I crept slowly up to the locks and moored above them. I didn't want to unload this stuff so I was lucky enough to find my mate Bernard, who lived at the bottom lock-house, ready to earn some extra money for doing it.

Handel refused to believe that *"Ling"* could carry 24 tons, despite the evidence of the gauging stick, and I had a job to get the full payment out of him.

After one more trip to Worcester there were no orders. Three Willow Wrens had been to the Porcelain and filled the wharf up. How they got in on our contract still remains a mystery. The others relaxed with their laying money but I was in no mood to hang about. I called in at Holly Bank and put in a load for the G.E.C., telling George to sort the rate out with Handel. After unloading I caught the bus to town and walked round to our office in Bridge Street.

Handel told me off for using my initiative but I took no notice.

"A least I got a good rate for that job" he enthused. "6s a ton!"

"H'm. I used to get 6s 9d when I had my own boat."

Handel was furious. "Well, we all know how clever you are, don't we?"

One of the Traffic Inspectors was in the office and didn't help matters.

"Well, he must be a bit cleverer than you, Handel, if he got 9d a ton more."

The upshot was that I had to do several more trips to the G.E.C. even after our own traffic recovered which didn't suit me at all and it was only after some of the other Captains expressed a desire to do it that I was able to return to my favourite waters. At this time there was a lot of milk powder traffic about. It came in two varieties of packing, big crates or paper bags. With the crates the hold was full with 16 tons but it was possible to get 20 or 21 tons on with the bags.

Cleaning the hold for paper bags was difficult. Well, it was easy enough to get it clean but not to get it dry, the false floors were always soaked through from the water in the coal and getting them dry was a problem. Back in the old days, boats carrying coal on the Worcester cut would take up their false floors, stack them in the fore-end and load the coal on the main bottoms. We didn't do this, shovelling on a surface obstructed by knees was a nuisance and, in any case, most of our back loading came in wooden boxes so a bit of damp underneath didn't hurt. Once again, in former times, depots would have a few bales of straw to spread over the floors if necessary but there was nothing of the sort at Worcester.

The next break in the routine was when I was asked to go to Gloucester. They were starting to take up some of the redundant railway track in the dock and some had been bought for use as rubbing guards to protect the brickwork along the B.C.N. There was no agreed rate for Gloucester to Birmingham and we settled on 8s per ton.

After unloading at Worcester it only took four hours to drop down the river to Gloucester. Gloucester Quay is an awkward place to moor singlehanded because the river there is too narrow to wind the boat so that the fore-end stems the current. It was a matter of leaping off with a strap and making fast to a bollard on shore. The current brought the boat alongside so the fore end could be secured. Just in case the engine decided to 'go out' during this crucial manoeuvre, failure to accomplish which would mean drifting down onto Llanthony weir, I attached the half hundred-weight log to the line and kept it handy on the counter to act as an anchor.

My arrival at Gloucester caused some excitement because long boats had become a rarity there. All sorts of old boatmen appeared as if from nowhere and I was presented with a quantity of canvas fire hose which we used for making the scrubbed, white belt over the cratch. The next day, 21 tons of old railway lines was loaded into the boat, the dockers did this, and I was finished early enough to start back. There were a couple of feet of 'fresh' in the river, which meant working the slacks, and the journey to Worcester took seven hours. It felt more like 17 hours, the Severn, as seen from a loaded long-boat is a seemingly unending vista of high banks lined with trees and there was not much else to see. Diglis locks were closed for the night, or at least I couldn't find a lock keeper, so I had to tie up there.

The rails were destined for the British Waterways maintenance depot at the Sneyd, near Bloxwich on the Wyrley cut. This was conveniently close to the colliery but Handel had decided that *"Ling"* should have a repaint so instead I took her to Saltley via the Bar Lock where I had to change all my cabin things over to the *"Ford"*, an ex British Railways, Yarwood built boat, one of a number that had found their way into British Waterway's hands, both as carrying and maintenance craft. The reason for this was that *"Ling"* had been selected to star in a forthcoming Boat Show at Birmingham. Meanwhile I was to be towed about by Vern Nixon.

I enjoyed my short time on *"Ford"*. It's amazing how dirt-engrimed hands eventually become clean once you are away from a motor boat! She was very light to steer but it wasn't possible to get more that 24 tons on her because of her shallow hold. As usual, though, I couldn't be anywhere near a National engine without it breaking down, and sure enough, *"Severn Dolphin"* failed going out to the colliery and we had to tie up at Benny's (Little Bloxwich). Once again it was the oft encountered failure of the combustion top becoming loose, hitting the cylinder head and smashing the piston.

After a couple of days delay, fortunately we were tied right outside a pub, we loaded and set off for Worcester, stopping for a night at Wolverhampton and going from there to the top of Tardebigge. I had wondered what it would be like going down Tardebigge locks but, in the event, there was no problem. Once we got through the Engine Lock, after which the locks were close together, Vern went ahead, starting the locks filling behind him. We used to do this by drawing a bit of paddle as the boat was going out of the lock, the steerer standing by the bottom gates, starting one with his hand and the other with a shaft before jumping down onto the moving boat. The force of the water did the rest!

I had rigged up a block rope so as to start *"Ford"* out of the empty locks more easily. She steered herself down the pounds without any problems. When I got to the top gate of the lock below, by this time already full, I opened it. As the fore-end entered the lock, I drew a bit of bottom paddle to suck her in, stood by the bottom gate and strapped it to stop the boat and close the gate which slammed to under the force of the partly drawn bottom paddle. In this way we got down the locks in fine style.

We needn't have hurried. It was the Easter Bank Holiday and we weren't allowed to unload so we tied in the basin. I had a visit from Rose and Joe Skinner accompanied by a young lady I knew from Coventry. Going back our departure was delayed, Vern being convinced he was onto a sure thing with a lady he had met in the Shades public house. We spent lunch time in there, but she didn't put in an appearance. There was a strong wind onto the towpath going back which made bow-hauling the butty difficult and eventually we stopped half way up Tardebigge locks.

Back in Birmingham I found that Joe Safe had brought *"Ling"* up from Saltley and I was told to cloth her up, make some white top-strings and buy a new beret. However, I lived on the *"Ford"* while the boat show was on, just standing by my motor during the day to talk to visitors. The show consisted of the *"Ling"*, a few British Waterways pleasure boats, an exhibition in a marquee and a refreshment tent.

It was the 16th May before I loaded again at 'Edgeford and I was down at Worcester with the Safes. We were held there for several days waiting for a load of copper for Sherborne Street and I took the opportunity to have a ride on a Stourport bound barge. She was *"Sabrina IV"*, captained by Fred Lyppiatt and the mate was a Scouse lad who sadly lost his life taking a Bristol sand dredger out to the Persian Gulf in the 1980s. *"Sabrina IV"* had lightened at Diglis before going up to Stourport. She was preceded in the tow by *"Sabrina II"*, captained by 'Cockers' Clutterbuck and the tug was the *"Severn Victor"* ('Twizzy' Spiers). When we came to the first lock I was interested in the procedure. Only one vessel could lock through at a time, the tug went first then pulled the first barge in using the long towrope. Once the first two vessels were above the lock the last barge could be pulled in in the same manner. I disembarked at Holt lock to catch an empty Regent's motor tanker back to Worcester.

This load of copper to Birmingham was to be my last on the *"Ling"*. We had been told some time before that the coal contract would end in April 1961 and the fleet would be disbanded.

Meanwhile, I had had the opportunity to make many contacts among the Severn bargemen and I was interested in going to work for the river fleet. I had consulted George Cox and he agreed to the transfer as soon as there was a vacancy. My last trip was an idyllic one. Leaving the Blockhouse early on a beautiful late May morning, I savoured the familiar Worcester cut scene, pausing at the Halfway for that reviving pint that would send me up the rest of the flight like a bat out of hell. It was quite early when I got through Shortwood tunnel but there is a lovely mooring there and I tied up and went for a swim in the clear water. I was sunbathing on the cabin roof when the Safes arrived and tied up with me. We all went into Birmingham and unloaded the next day. If only boating could always be like this! So ended my career as a canal boatman in the familiar surroundings of Sherborne Street wharf where I returned Joe's brass top pipe and gave all but a few of my plates and brasses to Polly.

CHAPTER EIGHT

Barging

British Waterways could be crafty and it was a condition of my transfer to the Severn Fleet that I should first do the holiday reliefs for the Severn lock-keepers. I didn't particularly want to do this and would have preferred a few more months on the *"Ling"* but I thought it was best to secure a job while it was available. The holiday relief lock keeper lived in a caravan which was towed from lock to lock as required. I was to start at Holt Lock and I arranged with the B.W. Road Services Superintendent, based at Sherborne Street, for a Worcester-bound lorry to drop me off there.

The locks at that time were manned by two men. The paddles were mechanised in those days, but not the gates. It's hard to believe but these lock-keepers worked seven days a week from 6am to 7pm. However, craft could come through at any time after hours providing they had booked to do so and the lock-keepers were paid 3s 6d for each craft out of hours. Unofficially they arranged one day off a fortnight on a Saturday by dint of one man doing two men's work. Saturday was a quiet day for barges whereas the bargemen all tried to work Sundays for the extra pay. On the Severn it was said, "Six days shalt thou labour, and on the seventh shalt thou go up and back." In other words, from Gloucester back to Gloucester.

The basic wage for the relief lock-keeper was around £11 per week, about the same as I was earning with *"Ling"*. I had no accommodation or gas costs to pay so it was profitable. George Woodward and Geoff Breakspear were the lock-keepers at Holt where I spent a month before moving to Bevere, or Camp Lock. While I was at Holt the *"Risca"*, a pleasure boat used by British Waterways to entertain its customers, came through. George Element was on board; when he spotted me I was greeted with the well remembered "Gor Blimey!" George Cox, in charge of the proceedings was more than a little inebriated and, seizing the wheel, steered an uncertain course out of the lock and down the river.

'Pinky' Brown presided over Camp Lock. In times of high water he would stand by the bottom gate and tell the bargemen that, as long as the highest place on their barge was below the height of his cap, they had enough headroom under Worcester bridge. While I was here, Vern Nixon and Gordon Beck, who had taken over the "*Ling*", came down with two loads of tinned fish from Stourport and stopped there for the night. It was at Camp that I met an old boatman in the pub who could recall taking long boats down the Severn between Gloucester and the entrance to the Stroudwater canal at Framilode, using the tide and a sail.

The next lock to be relieved was Diglis, where there were two locks, both equipped with electric capstans. The gates on the big lock were extremely heavy to open and close. Queues of barges built up her around midday as the smaller and faster Regent's tankers starting from Sharpness caught up with the much slower Harker's tanks and the British Waterways tugs starting from Gloucester. There was, at this time, an enormous amount of traffic on the Severn. British Waterways had to hire extra barges from various Bristol Channel carriers and the wharf at Diglis often worked Sundays and even Bank Holidays. It was while at Worcester I bought a Vespa scooter which was useful as the next lock I went to was two and a half miles outside town.

The last lock on which I did reliefs was Upper Lode, near Tewkesbury. John Jones was the lock keeper. His brother worked on Tewkesbury railway station. It is a big lock, capable of accommodating one of Harker's big tankers as well as a tug and two barges at the same time. The gates were opened by winches and could be started shut by a block and tackle attached to the balance beams. Mains power had to be converted to DC to operate the paddles. The lock was so long that we used bicycles to go from one end to the other. In this lock, dumb barges had to be stopped by the lock keeper using a rope thrown ashore from the barge.

There was a large field below the lock full of mushrooms. There were so many that you could pick them in the dark. Half a mile downstream was the Lower Lode pub. On a weekday night I would usually be the only customer and would be invited into the landlady's parlour.

At long last the period of lock relieving came to an end. I had a phone call from Albert Webb, who had replaced Mike Lovesey as Fleet Superintendent, to tell me I was appointed mate on *"Sabrina 3"*, Captain Harold Whitmore. She was at Avonmouth and I was told to be at Gloucester at 1 pm the following day to hitch a ride to Avonmouth on the MB *"Severn Stream"*, Captain Bertie Eglinton. I had already bought a caravan sited at Church-down to live in.

Dismounting from my scooter at Gloucester Docks in good time, I was directed to a café outside the docks to get a meal before we sailed. There was a regular down convoy at 1 pm for vessels sailing from Sharpness on the evening or night tides. Each convoy was accompanied by a passman who cycled from Gloucester to Purton opening the towpath side of the swing bridges which were double leafed at that time. The journey down the canal took three hours due to the six mph speed restriction so the engine just ticked over all the way down.

Being completely ignorant of tidal working I was surprised when we tied up at Sharpness but it was explained to me that we could not lock out until two hours before high tide, or "flow" as it was locally called. The mast, which carried the masthead navigation light and a derrick boom, had to be raised. It was dark when we untied and joined the rest of the barges jostling for the lock. Outside in the estuary it was pitch black except for the lights on shore. At that stage, of course, I could not distinguish the navigation lights from the others. It was exciting to be travelling on these strange waters in the dark. The mate made a meal and we ate on the way down. In a couple of hours we arrived at Avonmouth and locked up into the docks and shortly afterwards we moored alongside *"Sabrina 3"* and I was introduced to my new captain, Harold. Harold was a small elderly man who walked with a slight limp. He turned out to be a congenial character and an ex- Grammar School boy like myself and had a vast knowledge of barging. We went inside the wheel-box which was large and roomy. A hatchway, protected by a raised coaming, projected into the wheel-box by which access was gained, by a vertical ladder into the cabin. To the left of the ladder was a coal range of the size fitted in canal boats. There were two bunks, two seats, a table, a food cupboard and two clothes lockers. I was shown the forward below decks space where the intricacies of the marine toilet were explained to me. This space also contained the anchor chain bin and various stores and bits of equipment. I was told that we were tied up at a part of the docks known as 'starvation corner' because it was the furthest point away from the gates or canteen.

The six *"Sabrina"* barges had been built in 1944 by Charles Hill of Bristol for the Ministry of Food and were originally ,managed by the Severn Carrying Company which was nationalised in 1948. The Ministry had also constructed two 'buffer depots' around the same time, one at Worcester and one at Stourport. The idea of these buffer depots was that food stocks could be widely distributed and stored around the country, away from the port areas which were particularly susceptible to air raids. The *"Sabrinas"* were, in my opinion, some of the best dumb barges ever designed. They were about 90 ft long and 20 ft beam and could carry 150 tons on a draught of 6ft which was the summer level in the river Severn above Worcester. Their big advantage over other designs was the hatches. These were laid fore and aft on moveable beams. The beams could be lifted slightly by a portable roller jack that enabled them to be moved out of the way when working cargo. The more usual and much more awkward hatch design was to have fore and aft beams between the athwartships beams. You had to balance on the cross beams to lift out the fore and aft beams with the danger of falling in the hold. The hatch boards on these barges were laid athwartships.

The following morning a tug came and placed us alongside a ship from which we loaded sugar for Gloucester from where it was delivered as required to a jam factory at Ledbury. The loading was performed by dockers, all we had to do was to make sure the barge was properly trimmed. The "*Sabrinas*" had to be one inch deeper at the stern than at the bow to be able to steer them. If one was seen which was not properly trimmed Harold would say that it looked like a 'pig going grunting'. Loading completed, all we had to do was roll the beams into position, replace the hatch boards which had been piled up on deck, sheet them up and secure the sheets by steel battens held in place by wooden wedges. The hold was now completely watertight and could withstand the waves which, in rough weather, might wash right over us.

The "*Sabrinas*" had been built to go down channel as far as Cardiff and there were wires which could be fastened across the hatches for greater security but we never went below Avonmouth so had no need to use these. On top of the hatches went the two tow ropes at the front of the hold with a 'stopping rope' at each corner all neatly moused down.

At four hours before high water the tug "*Primrose*" came to collect us and we joined three other dumb barges in the lock. Four barges was the maximum tow. They might not be all British Waterways craft; barges belonging to private firms were also towed. There was a ship in the lock and the rest of the space was filled with barges, dumb and motor.

We towed in the Severn estuary, or 'outside' as it was called, using the thicker of our two tow ropes. I was shown how to take a turn round the king post right in the bows and make the rope fast on two bitts on the forward deck. These bitts had flat tops and were situated just where you might walk into them when hurrying forward in the dark. I had many a bruised shin from these. The first steering length, from Avonmouth to Charston Rock is traditionally the captain's. Before you get to Charston you go through the 'Shoots', a narrow channel between submerged rocks where the tide runs fast and there are sinister looking whirlpools. Then I was given the wheel for the next length. The wheels on the "*Sabrinas*", as on all the dumb barges working the upper river were small. They had to be as they were the highest point on the barge when it was stripped down to go under bridges in times of flood. Being small they had to be low geared so there were twelve turns of the wheel from hard a port to hard a starboard. The wheel was connected to the rudder by worm gear which is not an ideal mechanism because it has a lot of friction. You couldn't steer using the spokes but instead had to sit on a stool and wind the wheel using a handle projecting forwards from the rim.

At Sharpness the tug turned head to tide and we waited for the signal permitting our entrance to be hoisted. There was a crowd of motor barges waiting to go in with us. I had to go forward and take in the heavy towrope, we didn't try to pull it in hand over hand but walked back along the deck with it. Normally we would be locked up in the lock but occasionally the Harbourmaster would decide to 'make a level' which meant filling the tidal basin as well. This took a very long time which was not pleasing because we were being paid by the trip.

Depending on the time of our arrival we might be able to go straight up to Gloucester or might have to spend the night at Sharpness which is quite a small place with three pubs and no cinema. The voyage up the canal normally took about three hours and we were towed by one of the 'outside' tugs, either the "*Primrose*", "*Resolute*" or "*Addie*". Another tug, the "*Stanegarth*", was also used in the canal. If we were very unlucky we might have a string of timber lighters loaded at Sharpness added to the tow which would slow us down considerably. The barge was always scrubbed off going up the canal to get rid of the mud laden estuary water which washed over the decks. This had to be done by dropping a bucket on a rope over the side, sloshing water over the decks and scrubbing them with a deck brush. The decks were of 'diamond plating' to make them less slippery and the mud used to collect in the 'diamonds'. The approach to Gloucester was heralded by a timber pond, extensive canal side timber yards and the oil dock at Monks Meadow. Later another oil wharf was constructed at Quedgeley. On arrival at Gloucester we nearly always tied up for the rest of the day because the upriver tugs usually left early in the morning.

On this occasion our cargo was destined for Gloucester and we unloaded into one of the single story warehouses on the west side of the dock. Ahead of us the MB *"Severn Trader"* was discharging match splints and carpets. We had to put the slings on the heavy bags of sugar ourselves. When you have finished unloading a sugar barge you are sticky all over including your hair. Then we went 'light ship' to Avonmouth and loaded spelter for Worcester.

The average wages on the dumb barges were £14 per week but around this time the men instituted a 'work to rule', refusing to work barges on Sundays. This drastically cut earnings so I was fortunate to be given the job, which no-one else wanted, of going to Worcester to look after the barges moored there during the weekend, a job that had to be done because the river was in flood. The 'go-slow' didn't last long and the management were able to persuade us to agree to an arrangement whereby, instead of working only one barge, each crew would be responsible for two. In practice it worked out that, when our 'home' barge was delayed we would work *any* barge needing to be moved. Earnings shot up to £17 per week and, in one memorable week I earned £31 before tax.

It's time to mention the other barges in our fleet, or rather two fleets. Yes, believe it or not, British Waterways had to have two fleets of barges. We were Number One Fleet. Number Two Fleet consisted of three barges, the *"Pyramid"*, *"Pinkabolic"* and *"Lufa"*, formerly belonging to a firm called Cook's. Cook's bargemen were registered dockworkers and paid on an entirely different scale than those of us in the other fleet. Also in this fleet was a 400 ton Belgian barge, the *"Toujours Pret"*. She had a horizontal steering wheel and, because of her size, the union required her to be manned by four men, which was really quite unnecessary. I only saw her used once, as a timber lighter from Sharpness to Gloucester.

In our own fleet we had, as well as the six *"Sabrinas"*, four C/S barges, short for Channel/Stourport. They had been built after nationalisation by an aircraft firm in Anglesey and were real monstrosities. With inadequate run aft and 36 turns on the wheel they were almost impossible to steer and always had to be hung on the tug first so that there would be another barge behind to steady them. Otherwise they were similar to the *"Sabrinas"* except for having light aluminium hatch boards. An unpleasant feature, which would not be tolerated by the Health & Safety authorities today, was the absence of stanchions and chains to prevent anyone from falling overboard. Instead a wire was strung along the port side of the coamings. Nobody ever wore life jackets in those days and to slip off the deck into the swirling waters of the estuary meant almost certain death. There were also three *"Bird"* barges, *"Severn Falcon"*, *"Severn Eagle"* and *"Severn Hawk"*. These had slightly smaller cabins and smaller wheelboxes and the inconvenient type of athwartships hatch covers. Both the C/S and the *"Bird"* barges could carry more than a *"Sabrina"* being much more lightly built and not allowed below Avonmouth. British Waterways had just taken over the 'outside' barges of Chadbourn, Mousell & Co, leaving them to retain their large fleet of timber lighters. These were quite small craft with high coamings. I saw one once loaded with 130 tons and the water was over the deck amidships. They had tiller steering with no protection for the helmsman and also had no chains and stanchions. Fortunately I managed to avoid ever having to work one of these.

The worst disadvantage to the new system of working was being sent to Avonmouth on day- work to hatch and unhatch barges and supervise their loading. This meant travelling on what was known as the 'second mail', a train which left Gloucester at about 4.30 am. To get to Avonmouth you changed at Bristol Temple Meads. You wouldn't get home until about 8 pm. All this for a flat day's wage and no travelling time. Fortunately this didn't happen very often.

One job I enjoyed was to travel to Stourport and sling the cargo on an unattended barge, unloading at the Alcan Aluminium wharf there. After unloading, someone would give me a hand to roll the beams back into position and I could then hatch the barge up myself. Regent's tankers left Stourport at hourly intervals in the afternoon and I would hitch a tow behind one down to Lincomb Lock, lock my barge through, and then tow behind the next tanker to Holt fleet and so on down the river. On one occasion I got right back to Gloucester before the tug. Being towed short up on cross straps I could go on board the tanker and have a steer.

Barging was quite different from boating. It was an easy enough job with a crew of two and well paid. I liked the appearance of our "Sabrina", deep loaded with hardly any freeboard, looking clean and neat and tidy. There were no dirty cargoes and the hold was always dry. When you were steering you could have a portable radio on in the wheelbox. There was plenty of time for cooking and eating and there was a subsidised dock canteen at Avonmouth and cheap eating places round the docks at Gloucester. But I missed the hell-for-leather working of the narrow canals, river barges were ponderous things and locking was comparatively slow. The other crews were very congenial, easy going men. Most of them were from Gloucester but we had one lad from Liverpool and the skipper of the MB "Severn Side" was a Scotsman with a deep sea master's ticket.

Only twice did we depart from our usual route. On one occasion we went up the Bristol Avon to the City docks. We were towed by the *"Severn Stream"*, these trips to Bristol being the only time our motor barges got to use their tow hooks, and we loaded wood pulp, destined eventually for British Industrial Plastics at Oldbury, from a Canadian ship. Loading with us were a number of Ashmead's barges for the board mills further up river.

Another time we loaded big logs for Lydney. The tug towed us up to outside Sharpness then went straight across to Lydney docks from where we were towed up the Lydney canal to the plywood factory by a small motor launch. We had to leave our home barge here for unloading and go back to Gloucester on the train.

It was while I was working on these barges that I renewed my acquaintance with Jeanne. She had a summer job at Lynton and we arranged to meet for a day at nearby Barnstaple. This was a major train journey in those days starting at 4:30 am on the 'second mail', changing at Bristol and Taunton and completing the journey across Exmoor on the remote and beautiful Taunton to Barnstable line. The return journey involved the 1:10 am mail from Bristol getting back to Gloucester about 2:15 am. We had a wonderful day and I decided to spend my summer holiday at Lynton.

At Lynton we really got to know each other. Love blossomed in that lovely place and, before returning to work, I had proposed and been accepted.

CHAPTER NINE

On the Tanks

I was still at that stage in life when I wanted to try something new, and what I wanted to do was to get on a British Waterways motor barge. Obviously it would be more interesting and I preferred making myself comfortable on one barge rather than constantly changing craft. However there was no immediate possibility of making this change so I decided to apply for a job on the Regent Oil Company tankers.

I had got to know some of the tanker men on the occasions when I had persuaded them to give me a tow and had found out something about the job. But when I went round to their office at Monk Meadow, the boss, Peter Clements, didn't seem eager to employ me, until I produced my R.A.F. discharge papers which did the trick. All the Regent's bargemen lived at Sharpness and I was also required to live there so I found a pitch on the Hook Farm caravan site at Berkeley. Also living on this site was an old friend, Billy Hatton, who had worked for Regent's but now had a job at the new Nuclear Power Station.

My first appointment was as Mate on the *"Regent Jill"*, captained by Brian Jones with whom I was acquainted. 'Mate', on the Regent barges, really meant 'boy', the Mate's functions being carried out by a Mate/Driver. The Driver was Ginger Prosser from Dursley. The *"Jill"* was one of their older barges with the cabin forward. The engine had a direct cooling system. The Severn estuary carried a lot of sediment so we had to remove the inspection covers once a week and scoop out the mud. When replaced these inspection covers always leaked. I was able to suggest a remedy and when we had smeared them with grease they were perfectly watertight.

After a few trips I was transferred and promoted to Mate/Driver on the *"Regent Robin"*. She was a modern barge, built around 1950 together with a sister ship the *"Regent Wren"*. Both were designed to work down as far as Swansea, but only in the summer months. Consequently she had a raised foc'sle that made steering her when empty difficult because of the obstructed view forward. She had a roomy engine room and spacious accommodation aft, consisting of the captain's cabin, a mess room with upholstered settees and a two bunk cabin for the crew.

The mate was a young man from Worcester who was very knowledgeable and brought a sextant to work with him. Not that we ever needed recourse to celestial navigation in the Severn estuary! We got on very well and would wind the skipper up outrageously. On meeting Brett for the first time he told me "We don't need to learn to handle this barge, we need to learn to handle the skipper". When the captain came on board he immediately told us, "I don't want any fiddling on this barge"... our faces fell... "unless I'm in on it".

'Fiddling' was endemic on the waterways and always had been. Back in the 1770s, the carrier Hugh Henshall was obliged to put supercargos on each of his boats going out onto the Trent because of the reputation of the Trent watermen for theft. On the narrow canals coal was always regarded as common property and the same attitude applied to petrol on the Severn. Every now and then someone was caught, sacked and reinstated three months later. Bargemen also went on board the ships at Avonmouth and acquired duty free cigarettes, spirits and other 'high purchase tax' items such as transistor radios, all of which commanded a ready sale up river.

I lost a good friend in a fiddling accident. He had gone back to his Harker's tanker one evening at Gloucester and had been filling some cans of petrol from the pump room. Overcome by fumes, he had been found dead when the crew arrived next morning.

The skipper was easygoing and we all got on well on the "*Robin*". The mate and I tried to wind our captain up with remarks to each other like "Pass the breadfruit, Mr Christian" but the allusion to Captain Bligh always passed unnoticed.

The routine on Regent's tankers when leaving Sharpness on a night tide was, if the river was calm, to tie alongside another barge for the journey to Avonmouth. When we did this, the Driver would turn in and would load the barge at Avonmouth while the rest of the crew slept. While the barge was loading we took the opportunity to clean the binnacle and other brasswork. The controls were mounted on a pedestal to the left of the wheel, a wheel for the throttle on the left of the pedestal and the gear change on the right. All these were of brass as was the siren plunger. Like the "*Sabrinas*", these barges had to be loaded an inch by the stern and, when the river was high, we were advised the draught to which we could load. However we could never let the cargo rise above the ullage bar in each tank. The cargo was distributed among the tanks by means of deck valves. When it got about a foot below the ullage bar we would shout "Five minutes!" to the man in charge of the shore valve who would then have time to reduce the inflow gradually.

There was a subsidised canteen, operated by Shell, which we were allowed to use and it provided excellent meals for a ridiculously cheap price.

Shortly before four hours to flow we would muster on deck, the boom across the oil dock would be opened, and we would proceed to the lock. There was always a race to be first with these tankers. It was important to be in the first lock at Sharpness so that the crew, who all lived there, could get home as soon as possible. Sometimes, if the tide was right we could take a short cut across the Saniger Sands from a point above the Inward Rocks to Berkeley Power Station. On one occasion we were doing this with the "*Swallow*" when I felt her dragging the bottom. I immediately wound off all the power but there was no response to the throttle because it turned out that the Skipper was in the engine room adjusting the track rod for extra speed!

It was risky to do this because the cylinder head temperatures would rise and might put the temperature gauge needle through a 'gate' which would prevent it going back when the heads cooled. The gauge was sealed, you had the choice of leaving the needle in the gate or breaking the seal and resetting it. Either way you were on a loser because the fitters at Gloucester would check the engine every week and discover you had been driving the engine above its designed speed. Personally never interfered with the track rod but many hard driving skippers would 'put the spanner on' it if they were in a hurry.

One occasion when disaster was narrowly avoided was when we were one of a pair of empty tankers tied abreast and on our way down to Avonmouth. One of the skippers had brought a friend along for the trip. Below Berkeley he went below, leaving his friend in the wheelbox. Our own skipper, looking across and seeing someone in the wheelbox of the other barge, thought it was that barge's skipper and went below himself. The two barges were now proceeding without anyone to steer them. As was the custom, myself and the Driver of the other barge were turned in on our respective craft. I was shocked out of sleep by a nasty scraping noise and rushed up on deck, to be quickly joined by the other Driver, both of us with our shirt-tails flapping in the breeze. It turned out that we had just scraped over a ledge of rock known as Hill's Flats. Had there been a little less depth of water we would probably have ripped the bottoms out of them. No damage being apparent, we kept quiet about the incident and got away with it.

Regent's barges usually left Sharpness at hourly intervals in the morning so as not to wait for a turn on the discharging jetty at Stourport, the first barge leaving at 5 am. Going up the canal the Mate would scrub the main deck but the Driver would scrub the raised after deck. The canal was divided into three steering lengths. At Gloucester someone would get off at Llanthony Bridge, get any necessary shopping and rejoin the barge at the lock. There was a useful slot machine on the corner of Llanthony Road which dispensed cartons of milk.

Leaving Gloucester lock the skipper steered the tricky length up the Parting, narrow, winding and with many blind bends. The Mate then steered to Haw Bridge and the Driver thence to Upper Lode lock. Entering these lock cuttings you headed up to the point of the island and let the barge drop down at the last moment. Above Upper Lode the Skipper steered to Sandy Point, the mate to Clevelode and the driver to Diglis. Diglis to Camp Lock was the Skippers length, the Mate had her to Holt Lock and the Driver to Lincomb from where the Skipper took over and put her on the berth. Sometimes shore power was used for discharging, sometimes the barge provided power. On the *"Robin"* we had a Ruston diesel for pumping tanks, the other barges had an electric pump. The Ruston was identical to the auxiliary engine, known as the 'jenny', in the engine room and these were exactly the same as the Ruston engine I had had in the *"New Hope"*.

Unloading took about an hour and we would go back empty either to Worcester, Upton or Upper Lode. On one occasion we spent a night at Stourport. There was an unattended barge moored at Nelson Wharf. We suspected it was loaded with tinned tomatoes so we made our way down the badly eroded towpath to investigate. Our surmise was correct and we opened up the hold and extracted a case. We were soon staggering back along the difficult path in the pitch dark with a half hundredweight case. Exhausted from the struggle we relaxed in our cosy mess room. The skipper looked morose.

"What's the matter, Skip?"

"I was just thinking, why didn't we get another case while we were at it?"

In winter it was dark after we left Stourport so we rigged up portable headlights, two car lights on a board screwed to the for'ard bulwarks, adjusted so that one shone on the left hand bank and the other straight ahead. Going down in the dark with a steaming mug of tea at hand was fun but we also had fun in the long summer evenings, watching the fishermen scramble up the bank to escape our wash. There was a story, almost certainly the product of an overheated imagination, that an empty barge sucked all the water away from a young lady who was bathing in the river, revealing her in a state of total undress.

Some of the Regent skippers were keen "doggers" who liked to go ashore and see if they could spy on courting couples. Other bargemen had better things to do and could be seen hanging about outside the Nurses Home at Worcester. One or two adventurous girls would frequent the places where the barges moored at Worcester in the evenings.

Working for Regent's was pleasant enough but we had to spend a lot of time away from home. To get a whole Saturday at home it was the custom for either the Skipper or the Driver to take turns working the barge singlehanded between Sharpness and Gloucester or in the reverse direction. The crewman who was not working would drive his mate to Gloucester or collect him from there. This was forbidden both by the canal bye-laws and by Regent's but everyone knew it went on and nothing was ever said. It was exciting to be in sole charge of a tanker and to execute the tying -up manoeuvre singlehanded.

Regent's barges were smart craft and we were always scrubbing, polishing and touching up the paint. They were painted light grey with green pipe work and valves. We always regarded ourselves a something of an elite among rivermen.

Because of holiday reliefs and maintenance I worked on most of Regent's barges. I still suffered from hay-fever so, when volunteers were called for to work on the *"Robin"* or *"Wren"* during the summer months when they traded to Cardiff and Swansea (Regulations required them to have a crew of three for this work) I jumped at the chance. We loaded at Avonmouth for these destinations and, when on this job, would be away from home a whole week.

Occasionally the weather was rough and we would have to put canvas covers on the hatches giving access to cabin and engine-room which meant we had to remain in the wheelbox and forgo our mugs of tea and meals until the seas eased off. I didn't mind, a whole week in a pollen-free atmosphere was worth it.

Because we had to wait tides to depart from Cardiff and Swansea, it was possible to walk up to the city and do some shopping. In the case of Cardiff, this meant walking through Tiger Bay, a district which had a certain reputation but was really perfectly safe. Going down past the cliffs at Clevedon the skippers would be glued to their binoculars, hoping to see courting couples and passing on the highly embroidered results of their investigations to the man at the wheel.

In February 1962 Jeanne and I were married at her home at Enfield. Rose and Joe Skinner and Bert Dunkley came to the wedding. We spent our honeymoon in the Hotel Metropole at Blackpool before going to live in our caravan at Berkeley. Jeanne was soon expecting our first child, Robert, but we decided, because I was away for so much of the time, that it would be better if she went home to her parent's house for the birth. Robert was born in November.

It was fortunate we made this decision as we were soon plunged into one of the worst winters in living memory. The water system on our caravan site was an improvisation of rubber pipes which soon became frozen up. Roads were blocked by snow and trains were halted by snow in the points.

The canal became badly iced up. The local newspaper claimed it was four feet thick. I don't know whether this figure was accurate. Barges had to be formed into trains, each of which was assisted by a tug. Even the steam-powered tug, *"Mayflower"*, long tied up out of use, was pressed into service. The journey up the canal, usually accomplished in three hours, now took nine hours. It was possible to walk from one moving barge to another on the ice and we did this because the disruption to our schedules caused us to run out of fags, tea, bread etc. and we would try and buy some from another barge.

There was ice in the lock-cuts on the Severn as well. It would be two o'clock the following morning before we got unloaded at Stourport. Despite the struggle and delays the tankers kept up their weekly task of two trips a week to Stourport at the cost of almost continuous working.

In the estuary, a sort of icy sludge formed on the water. This got in the strum-boxes which filtered the cooling water and blocked them. We had to take the strum-box cover off and keep scooping out ice for much of the way going down. Coming back up, loaded, the inlet was well below the surface and there was no problem.

The big Harker and Shell barges that went to Swansea had another problem. Below Sharpness they had to erect their masts and radio aerial. When they arrived in the lock at Sharpness, all this rigging was festooned with long icicles and it all had to be chipped off before they could lower their gear to go up the canal.

Fortunately the thaw, when it came, was slow. A quick melt of all that snow would have caused flooding on the scale of 1947 when many of the Severn lock houses had several feet of water in them.

Now that we had a child, we had to think about buying a house and we looked at several, favouring a new one on the out-skirts of Gloucester. The price was about £3000 and I was earning £900 a year so it was well within our reach. Before we had em-barked on negotiations something happened that was to seriously disrupt our lives. My employers, the Regent Oil Company, told us that they were closing down their barge operations and would not be finding any shore jobs for the bargemen. This was in 1964, the close-down was a gradual affair which took place over several years.

I was in a quandary. I didn't want to hang on until the last minute and then find myself without employment. Harker's and British Waterways had vacancies for bargemen but they both told me that they didn't expect to be able to keep going for much longer. In the event, the last barge, except for Healing's grain barges trading to Tewkesbury, had disappeared from the Severn by 1970.

The trouble with watermen is that, like railwaymen, they have specific skills not of much use elsewhere in the labour market. In any case I knew I couldn't put up with factory work. A job on the railway would have been an obvious alternative but that industry was, at the time, laying off workers because of the Beeching cuts and the change-over from labour-intensive steam locomotives to diesel power.

The problem was solved quite neatly when I heard of a vacancy at Upper Lode Lock. Here was a job and a house! A visit to Mike Lovesey, who was then the Traffic Superintendent, got me the post. With great regret I bade farewell to my barge and we moved to Tewkesbury. It took me a very long time to get used to life ashore.

My generation were to be the last inland waterways boatmen.

EPILOGUE

Looking back on my boating days from the perspective of a long and varied life and a comfortable retirement, what are my thoughts today? By modern standards boatmen lived in poverty and yet we had everything necessary for a contented life. We walked lightly on the planet, owning only a few clothes, some bedding and basic cooking utensils. We didn't pay rent or taxes. Accommodation, heat and light cost us nothing. Our recreations were simple, a radio, the pub, the cinema, the fairground, the company of others of our ilk. We had the satisfaction of doing a real and vitally necessary job. What more could a young man want but a day of activity in the open air, a few pints of beer and a last contemplative cigarette and cup of tea before going to bed.

Life was far simpler and less stressful than it is today. Boatmen had no utility bills, Council Tax, nor the mountains of junk mail with which we now have to deal. The insatiable demands for charitable donations had yet to appear, all we needed to do, if we wished, was put some money in the Salvation Army tin and buy a poppy for Remembrance Day. Few people owned cars and most travelled only rarely. Outside the rush hour and holiday weekends, trains, infrequent by today's standards, were un-crowded and you expected, and usually got, if not a compartment to yourself, at least a corner seat.

Of course I enjoy all the luxuries of modern life, and particularly the opportunity to travel, but I sometimes feel we may have lost something along the way. Certainly, if I was a teenager just entering the world of work, I would have preferred it to be in the 1950's rather than today. There was not only full employment but stimulating occupations were available to the adventurous youth. This was a time when boys of seventeen were firing steam locomotives on the main line or fighting the east coast gales on the deck of a sailing barge. There was an air of freedom about life in general which is fast disappearing.

And what of the waterways themselves? Everything must change, and nothing material can stay the same. The waterways, which I experienced as a workplace, known to few except those of us who were involved in the water transport industry, have been transformed into a playground and a property developer's paradise. I am pleased to see people enjoying the new canals but I have no desire to join them and my present day interest is confined to waterway history. Confronted by monstrosities like the new canalside flats at Sherborne Street or the ugly buildings which have recently defiled Gloucester Docks I can only agree with the poet John Betjeman.

"For us of the steam and the gaslight, the lost generation,
The new, white cliffs of the city are built in vain."

'God gave us memories that we might have roses in December'. My memories of the cut are of the beat of a Bolinder heard far away across the fields or in the wintry afternoon haze of a canyon of grimy factories and wharves, an evening with other boatmen in a remote and old-fashioned canal-side pub, the cosy, almost womb-like atmosphere of a warm cabin.

Perhaps we should let Tom Rolt have the last word. In his book, "*Winterstoke*", a story of material change and its consequences, he wrote,

"Despite the contribution which the canal had made to the progress of industrial revolution, it had itself preserved the traces of an older, tougher and freer England which had everywhere been overwhelmed when the black tide swamped the green. To meet one of the long, narrow boats, glowing with barbaric colour and aglint with polished brass gliding slowly along the lonely levels on Barnby moors as dusk was falling was to be reminded, with a sudden pang of nostalgic anguish, with a sudden stirring of ancestral memory, of that lost England... A life of material poverty, hard, bitter often cruel and yet mysteriously enriched. By what?

By some brighter memory of lost Eden? As the reflected glow from its lighted cabin faded from the water, the traceless passing of the boat would recall the words of the gypsy, Petrulengo: 'There's night and day, brother, both sweet things; sun, moon and stars, brother, all sweet things; there's likewise a wind on the heath. Life is very sweet, brother; who would wish to die?" But now the canal was dead. The long boats would come no more to Winterstoke and, like the railway navvies before them, their people vanished without trace."

L T C Rolt, *Winterstoke*, Constable, 1954, quoted by permission of Mrs Sonia Rolt.

.

The Belmont Press, founded in 1948, specialises in *Waterways Publications* endeavouring to keep books in print, which may otherwise become unavailable to the collector and enthusiast alike.

The details on the following pages were correct at the time of publication

The 'Working Waterways' Series

This series was launched specifically to give a wider circulation to classic accounts, by men and women, who actually worked full-time on the waterways of England. They constitute the most authoritative record of a now vanished way of life - an invaluable source for waterways and social historians alike.

1) Maidens' Trip - Emma Smith
'Maidens' Trip' is a prize-winning book about women on narrowboats in the Second World War. This book is a lively and entertaining read, which bubbles with youthful high spirits. It tells the story of three girls working on England's canals during this period of time. 'Maidens' Trip' is part fact and part fiction, condensing experiences from across the canal world into a single, compelling read.

2) Troubled Waters - Margaret Cornish
A well-balanced account of wartime boating, recalling the pleasures and the problems thrown up by this extraordinary way of life. It was not written until 40 years after the war, which meant that the author could tackle her subject in a more honest, if less romantic, way than some of the earlier writers. It stands as an unvarnished tribute to that small group of girls who endured a variety of challenges to make their contribution to the war effort by crewing canal boats.

3) Bread Upon the Waters - David Blagrove
David started commercial boating in the 1950s and was thus able to witness and record the last years of long-distance narrow boat carrying on our canals. He was afloat during the disastrous 'Big Freeze' of the winter of 1962/3, which hastened the inevitable end of the commercial trade. Personal involvement makes this book an invaluable record of the canal world in the post-war years.

4) Idle Women - Susan Woolfitt

The ironic title of this book about the women canal-boat crews of the Second World War disguises the fact that, efficiently or otherwise, these women laboured hard under difficult conditions to shift essential wartime cargoes on England's canals. The author, second wife of the famous actor-manager, Donald Woolfitt, sought and found personal fulfilment in the arduous gritty life of the canal. Her unpretentious recollections of her adventures represent the first-ever description of this life from the inside - no one had ever before written from a first-hand experience of life carrying cargo on our canals.

5) The Amateur Boatwomen - Eily Gayford

By a series of chances, Eily Gayford started working on canal boats in 1941 and was thus well placed to become a trainer of the all-women crews established by the Ministry of War Transport the following year. As someone who had taken naturally to canal life herself she inspired a tremendous loyalty and devotion in many of her trainees. Her modest description of boating in the 1940s remains a unique record of the operation of this wartime canal scheme

6) Anderton for Orders - Tom Foxon

At the age of 17, Tom Foxon left an office job and ran away to the boats. This was in 1950 and young Tom was eager to experience life with working boatmen who still plied England's waterways, from London to Liverpool and from the Humber to the Bristol Channel. He was lucky to have been able to enter the world of canal carrying when he did, for it has now vanished. The colour and economic contribution of the canals of the time can be judged from listing some of the cargoes Tom met – Not just the traditional coal, gravel, grain and timber, but also borax, bentonite, nuts and bolts, dustbins, matches, canned tomatoes, wheelbarrows and even dates for making HP sauce! He writes with the enthusiasm of a teenager and with the keen eye of a canal aficionado, what a combination!

7) The Quiet Waters By - David Blagrove

David's first book ended in 1963 after the 'Great Freeze', but that didn't stop him boating. He went on to run a trip boat on the Kennett and followed this by a spell as a lock keeper. He recalls with wonderful detail his days with the Thames Conservancy, with its tradition of brass buttons and steam launches. The author still retained an interest in narrow boats and narrow boat carrying. He describes a number of memorable trips, including one that nearly ended in disaster, when floodwater swept him onto a weir. On a happier note, he tells us about the time he towed the Skinners' 'Friendship' to Stratford for the re-opening ceremony of the canal by the Queen Mother in 1964.

8) Hold On a Minute - Tim Wilkinson
The author tells how he and his wife hired a pair of boats from the Docks & Inland Waterways Executive in 1948, the forerunner of British Waterways, spending a memorable year carrying cargoes on England's canals.

9) Number One - Tom Foxon
In this, the sequel to *'Anderton for Orders'*, Tom Foxon is demobbed from the RAF and sets himself up in business as an owner boatman or 'Number One'. Before doing so he takes a memorable trip with a horse-boat from Tardebigge to Cannock and back to Worcester. His first few trips are plagued with engine troubles but, after replacing his National engine with a Ruston he settles down to recoup his fortunes by a winter spent on local work around Birmingham before starting to carry coal to Oxford.

10) Following the Trade - Tom Foxon
The third, and last, volume of Tom Foxon's boating trilogy finds him ranging widely over the waterways system as an owner boatman before selling up and working for British Waterways on the Birmingham- Severn route. With the loss of this contract imminent, Tom goes to work on a general cargo barge trading between Bristol, Avonmouth, Lydney and the river Severn before becoming a Mate/Driver on the smart motor barges of the Regent Oil Company with trips taking him as far afield as Stourport, Cardiff and Swansea.

This series will be added to as suitable material becomes available

Our Other Publications or Publications for which we hold the Rights –

ATHENE, ANATOMY OF A DREAM:Anthony H Lewis
BRITAIN'S CANAL AND RIVERCRAFT:E Paget-Tomlinson
CABIN CROCHET 1) Janet M Reeve
CABIN CROCHET 2) Janet M Reeve
CLOTHES OF THE CUT, THE:Avril Lansdell
COLOURS FOR CRUISERS:John M Hill
FROM STEM TO STERN:John M Hill
HIDDEN BOX, THE:Iris Bryce – A children's book
WALKING ON WATER:Nick Corble

Other Publications, which we distribute as wholesalers

AFLOAT IN AMERICA:Charles and A M Hadfield
ART OF THE NARROW BOAT PAINTERS, THE:A J Lewery
ARTERIES OF COMMERCE:GRAND UNION CANAL
BRITAIN'S CANAL AND RIVERCRAFT:E.Paget-Tomlinson
BRITISH CANALS:Charles Hadfield
CANAL LIFTS AND INCLINE PLANES OF THE WORLD:Uhlemann
CANAL RECOLLECTIONS:Julian Holland
CANAL:Anthony Burton and Derek Pratt
CANALS OF ENGLAND, THE:Eric de Mare
CHARLES HADFIELD,CANAL MAN AND MORE:Joseph Boughey
COMPLETE BOOK OF KNOTS AND ROPEWORK, THE:Eric C Fry
DECORATIVE FOLK PAINTING:Jean Payne
EXETER CANAL, THE:Kenneth R.Clew
EXPLORING ENGLAND BY CANAL:David Owen
FLOWERS AFLOAT:Tony Lewery
FROM SEA TO SEA:L.T.C.Rolt
GRAND UNIONS:Peter Ashley
GREAT TOWPATH WALK, THE:Brian Bearshaw
GREEN AND PLEASANT WALKS - CANALS OF THE MIDLANDS
INLAND CRUISERS - CARE & MAINTENANCE:Norman Alborough
INLAND CRUISING:Norman Alborough
INLAND WATERWAYS MANUAL:Emrhys Barrell
JAMES GREEN:CANAL BUILDER...:Brian George
JOHN GAGG BOOK OF 250 WATERWAY LANDMARKS
JOHN GAGG BOOK OF BROAD CANALS
JOHN GAGG BOOK OF NARROW CANALS
LANDSCAPE WITH CANALS:L T C Rolt
LOCOMOTION:200 YEARS/TRAIN TRAVEL:Ransom
LONDON AND SOUTH EAST ENGLAND:Martyn Denney
MONKEY MARSH LOCK (Kennet and Avon Canal)
NARROW BOAT PAINTING:A J Lewery
NARROW BOAT:L T C Rolt (HARDBACK)
OBSERVER BOOK OF BIRDS, THE
OBSERVER BOOK OF CANALS, THE:John Gagg
OBSERVER BOOK OF WILD FLOWERS, THE:Francis Rose
OLD FATHER THAMES AND SLEEPING BEAUTY:J Cook

PICTORIAL HISTORY OF CANAL CRAFT:Smith
PICTORIAL HISTORY OF CANALS:Gladwin
PORTRAIT OF THE RIVER TRENT:Peter Lord
PORTRAIT OF THE SEVERN:J H B Peel
RACE AGAINST TIME:David Bolton
RAILWAY DATA FILE, THE
RAILWAY PICTURE POSTCARDS:Maurice I Bray
RIVER AND CANAL TRANSPORT:John Vince
RIVER THAMES IN THE FOOTSTEPS OF THE FAMOUS:P Goldsack
RIVERS AND CANALS:Penny Marshal
RIVERS:Ronald Russell
SCOTLAND'S INLAND WATERWAYS:P J G Ransom
SECRET LIFE OF THE SEINE:Mort Rosenblum
SHROPPIE,A PORTRAIT OF THE:Thomas Pellow and Paul Bowen
SILVER HIGHWAY, THE:Malcolm MacDonald
SLOW BOAT THROUGH FRANCE:Hugh McKnight
SLOW BOAT THROUGH GERMANY:Hugh McKnight
SMALL BOAT IN THE MIDI:Roger Pilkington
STAFFORDSHIRE WATERWAYS:David Owen
SWEAT AND INSPIRATION:Martin Worth
TELFORD'S AQUEDUCTS,THOMAS (SUC):R Quenby
THAMES, THE:Paul Atterbury and Anthony Haines
THROUGH FRANCE TO THE MED:Mike Harper
THROUGH LONDON BY CANAL 1885:Arthur Lowe
TOUR OF THE GRAND JUNCTION CANAL 1819:Hassell and Cranfield
TOWPATHS OF ENGLAND:Brian Bearshaw
TRENT AND MERSEY CANAL:P Lead
UP THE CUT:Ivan E Broadhead
VICTORIAN AND EDWARDIAN BOATING/OLD PHOTOS:Neil Wigglesworth
VICTORIAN AND EDWARDIAN CANALS:Gladwin
VICTORIAN THAMES, THE:D.G.Wilson
WALKERS' OF RICKY:Anthony Walker
WALKING BRITAIN'S RIVERS AND CANALS:D Bellamy
WATERWAYS HERALDRY:Dennis Hadley
WATERWAYS RESTORED:Ransome
WATERWAYS SIGHTS TO SEE:Charles Hadfield
WILDLIFE:RIVERS AND CANALS:Hopkins and Brassley

    DEAN'S HISTORICAL WATERWAYS MAPS -
CANALS OF BIRMINGHAM
CANALS OF NORTH STAFFORDSHIRE
INLAND NAVIGATION – CANALS OF ENGLAND AND WALES
GRAND JUNCTION CANAL (1810)
LEOMINSTER CANAL (1789)
CANALS OF LONDON
CANALS OF MANCHESTER
MAP AND PROSPECTUS:MANCHESTER SHIP CANAL

The Working Waterways Series

This series gives wide circulation to the accounts of those who worked on England's waterways. The books form an authoritative record of a now vanished world - an invaluable source for waterways and social historians.

(All are A5 - Portrait, paperback)

1) Maidens' Trip by Emma Smith

2) Troubled Waters by Margaret Cornish

3) Bread upon the Waters by David Blagrove

4) Idle Women by Susan Woolfitt

5) The Amateur Boatwomen by Eily Gayford

6) Anderton for Orders by Tom Foxon – the first of his trilogy

7) Quiet Waters By by David Blagrove

8) Hold on a Minute by Tim Wilkinson

9) Number One by Tom Foxon – the second of his trilogy

10) Following the Trade by Tom Foxon – the last of the trilogy